Elementary Origami

An Introduction to the Taro's Origami Method

Taro's Origami Studio

ISBN-13 979-8-98-560290-6

Origami models and instructions are designed by Frank Ling, Jeff Raab, and Ben Friesen.

Taro's Origami Studio would like to give special thanks to Frank Ling and Jeff Raab for help with editing and diagramming.

Published by
Taro's Origami Studio
Suite #1100, 1628 JFK Blvd.,
Philadelphia, PA 19103
www.tarosorigami.com

Printed in USA

First printing February 2022

Introduction

Origami is the ancient art of paper folding. The word is Japanese, with "ori" meaning "to fold" and "gami" meaning "paper", but it began with the invention of paper in China nearly 1900 years ago. Today origami is designed, folded, and enjoyed all over the world and there are books, diagrams, and models published in every language.

Part of the appeal of origami lies in its simplicity, because all you need is paper. From there, the world of origami is as expansive as your imagination. Each fold gradually transforms an ordinary sheet of paper into beautiful flowers, elegant birds, mythological creatures, or anything else you can think of.

But origami also has applications that extend far beyond creasing paper. It has been used to develop everything from satellites and airbags, to skyscrapers, heart stents, and runway clothes. Origami techniques are quite useful when anything expands or contracts.

The benefits of origami for the folder are also numerous. As new folders begin, they develop skills like patience and precision, as well as the development of problem-solving skills, spatial relationships, cultural awareness, memorization, discipline, hand-eye coordination, and imagination.

With origami's surging popularity in recent years, more and more people are being hooked by this ancient art. At **Taro's Origami Studio**, a space dedicated to teaching and promoting origami, it is our mission to make origami accessible to folders of all ages. Taro Yaguchi founded Taro's Origami Studio in 2009 with a clear vision: First, to help people discover the thrills of origami and secondly, to establish a strong foundation so that each student can fold on their own.

It is our sincere hope that "Elementary Origami" starts folders of all ages on a lifelong path of folding, so that the wonderfully rich and rewarding tradition can continue to be passed down and the next wave of folders can take origami to even greater heights.

Contents

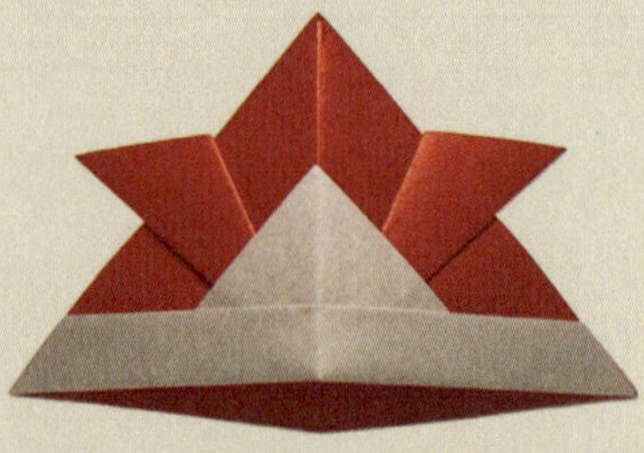

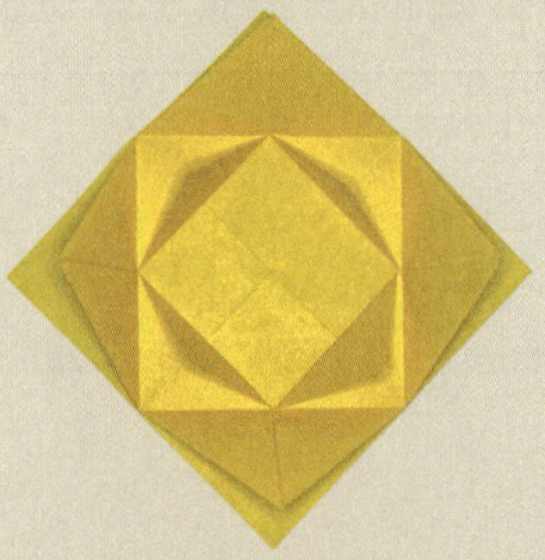

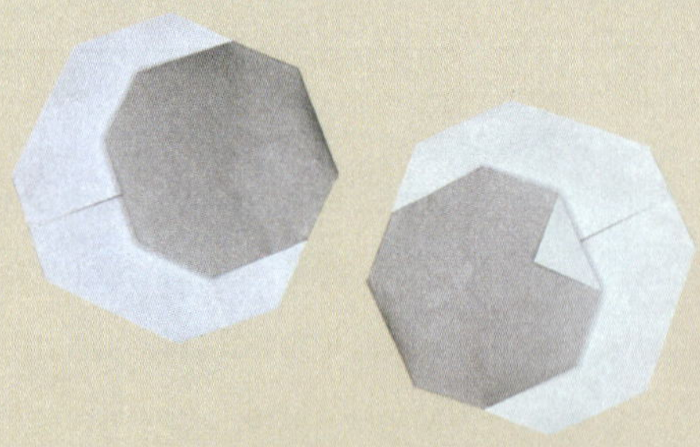

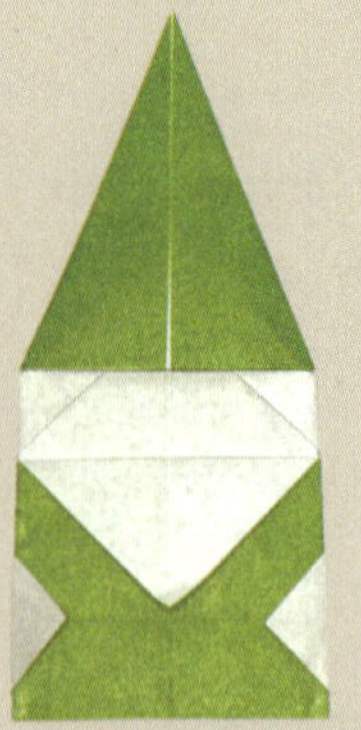

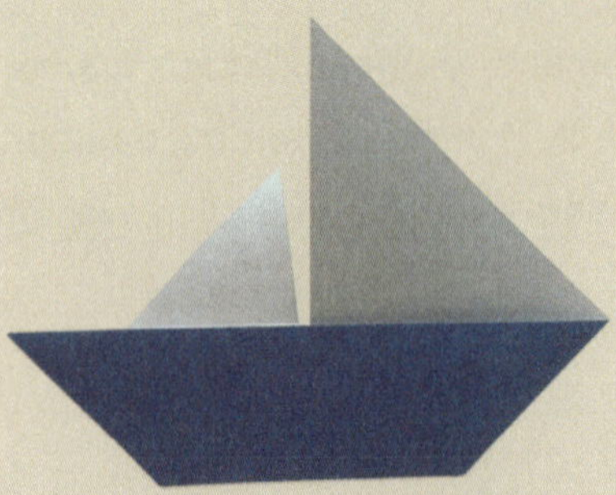

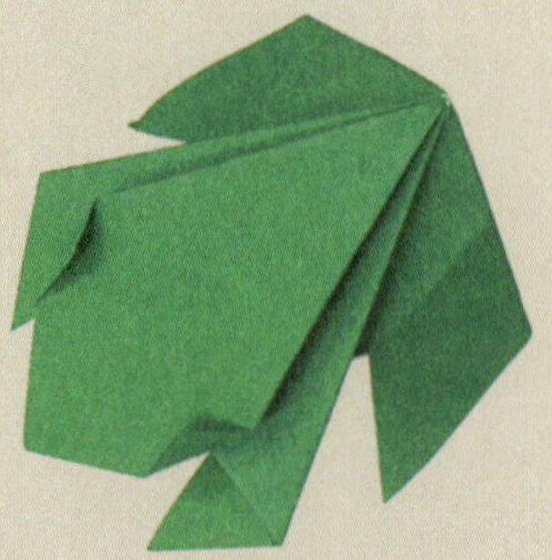

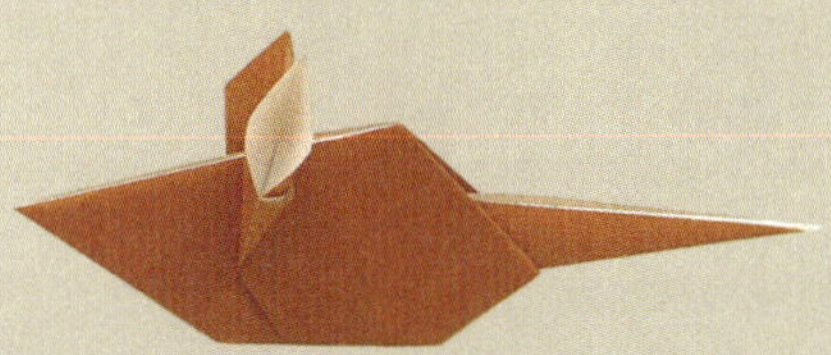

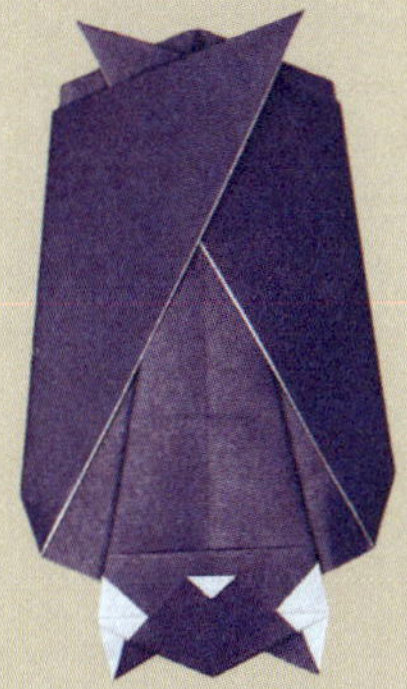

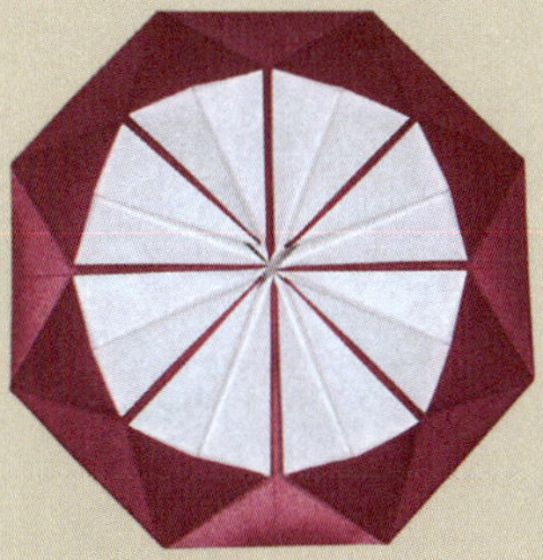

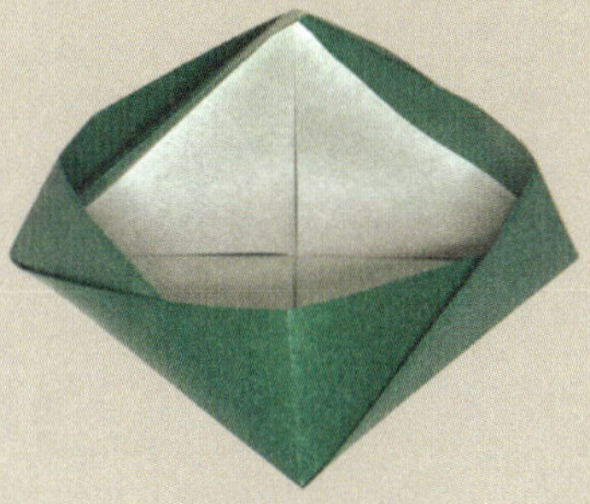

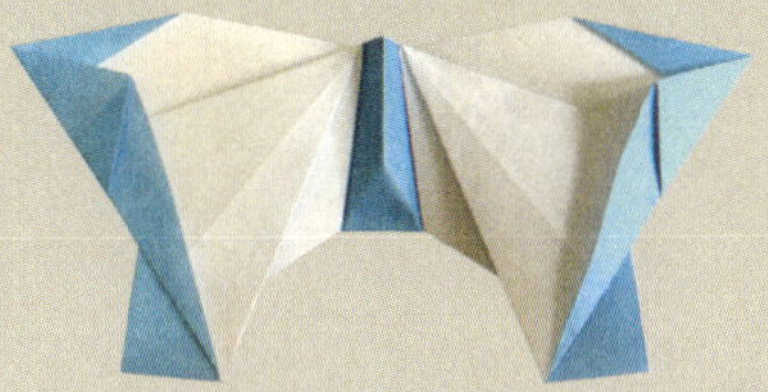

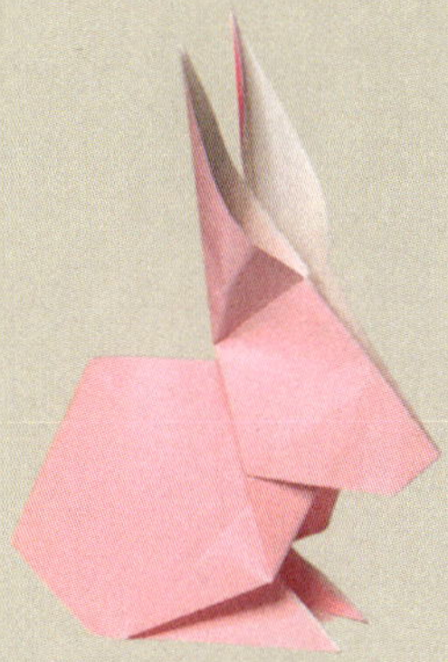

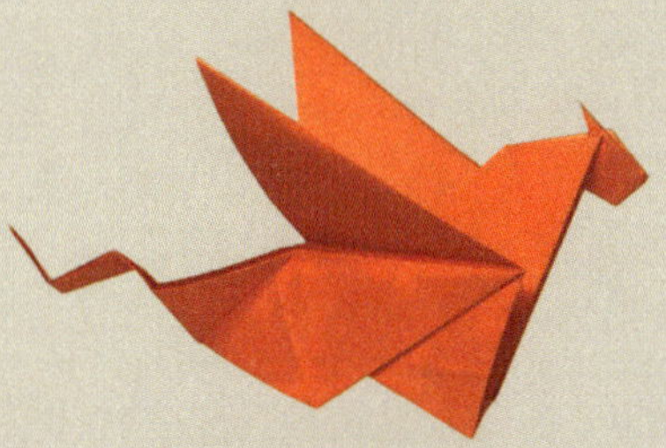

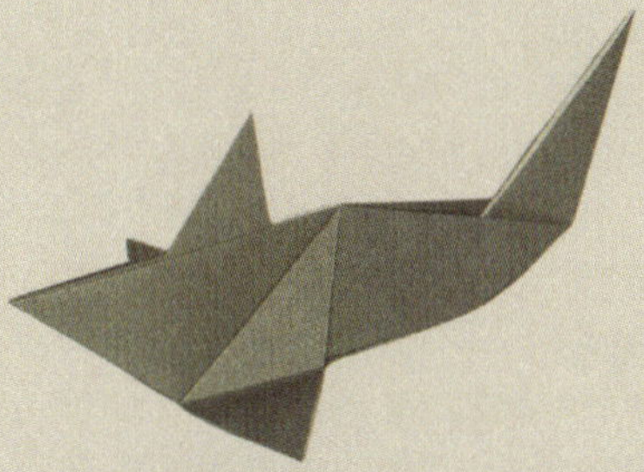

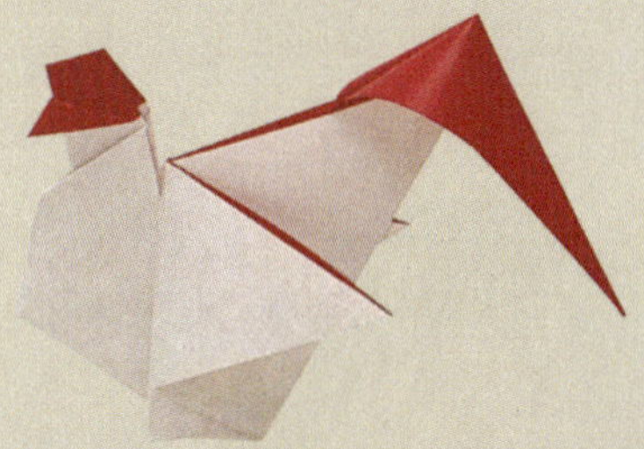

Meet the Artists

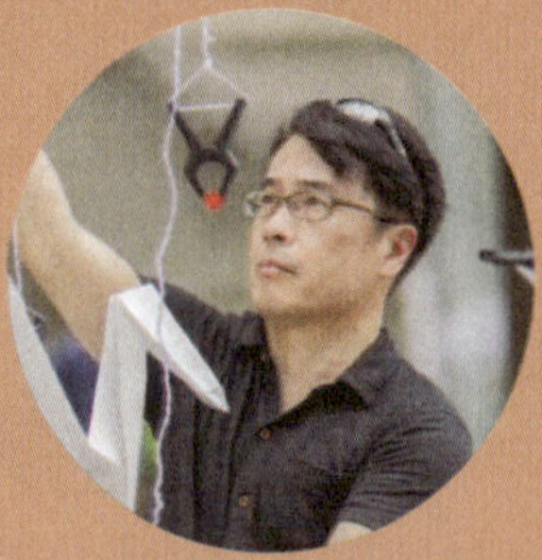

Taro Yaguchi

Taro founded Taro's Origami Studio in 2011 and has been on the forefront of helping promote paper-folding ever since. Today the studio is one of the premier places on the internet to learn origami, and their store is one of the largest places to find quality origami paper and books. He is also a gifted and prolific origami designer.

Models attributed: Rabbit

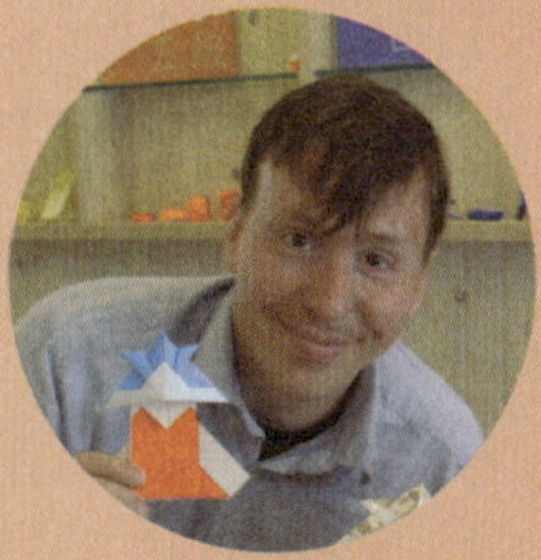

Ben Friesen

Ben has been folding and teaching origami his whole life and began working with Taro's Origami Studio in 2011. One of his favorite things in life is telling people that he folds paper for a living, becuase no one believes him. He designed the model in this book for his daughter, who loves bats and was born with one flapping around the house.

Models attributed: Sleeping Bat

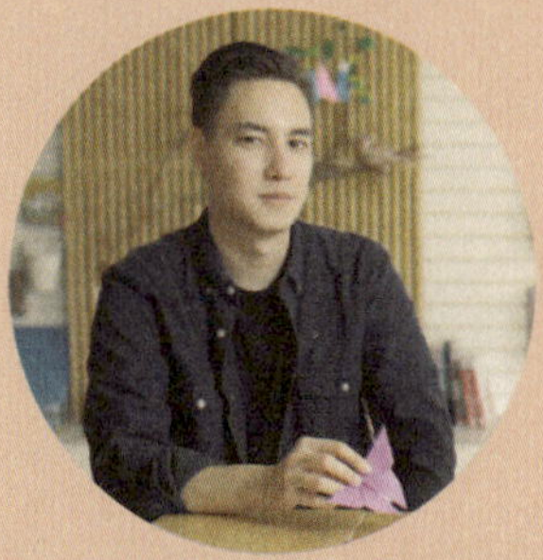

Frank Ling

Frank began his fascination with origami at a young age when his Grand-father folded a frog from a dollar bill. Joining up with Taro's Origmai Studio in 2012, Frank has been exploring every facet of paper folding and began designing his own models. Some of them are presented here in this very book (his personal favorite is the butterfly).

Models attributed: Sun(flower), Crescent Moon, Frog, Butterfly, Dragon, Shark, Rooster

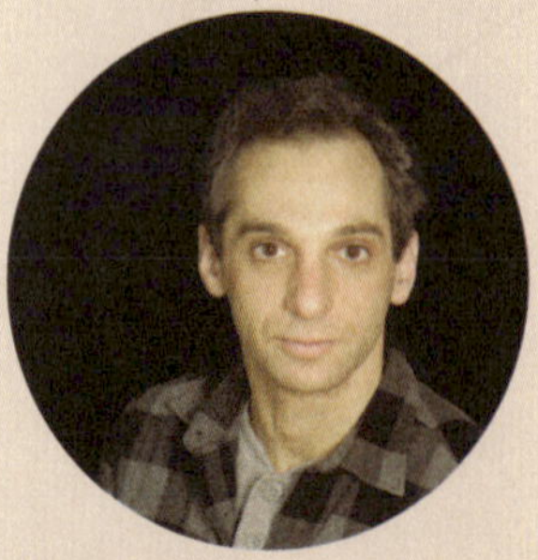

Jeff Raab

Jeff has been practicing origami for over 25 years, and began working with Taro's Origami Studio in 2014 as a teacher and artist. He has taught origami to students of all ages, led origami workshops with organizations all over the world, folded models for entertainment media, and provided in-person origami folding for events of all sizes. He is also a theater artist and musician.

Models attributed: Garden Gnome, Rooster

Symbols

Valley Fold

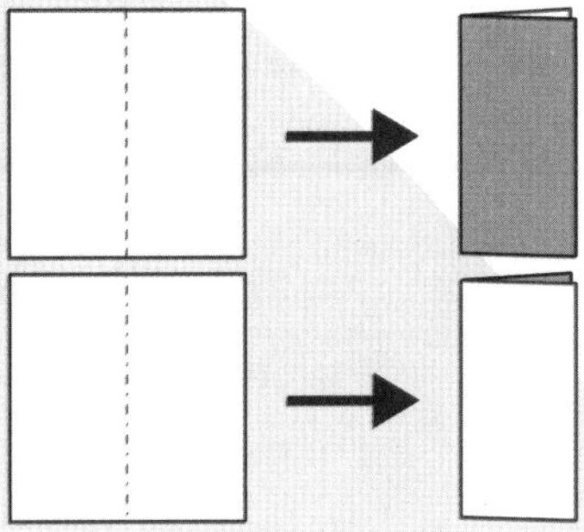

Mountain Fold

Fold in Direction of Arrow

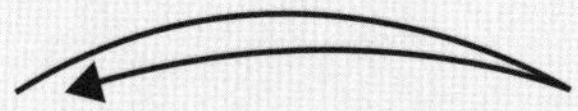

Fold and Unfold

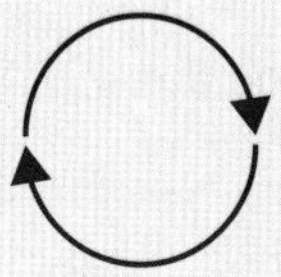

Rotate

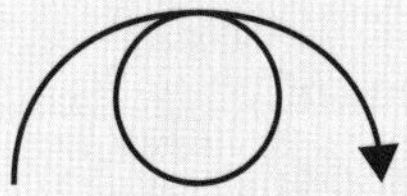

Turn Over

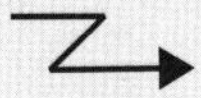

Pleat/Crimp

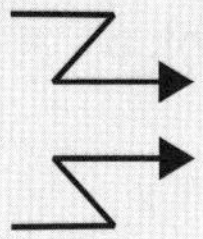

Inside Crimp Fold

Open

Taro's Origami Method

All origami begins with the same basic folds. Learning the precision and patience required to carefully complete them each and every time is an invaluable skill—one that is necessary for folders who wish to someday tackle the most complicated shapes and models.

At **Taro's Origami Studio**, we stress the fundamentals of origami so that everyone can develop their skills over time in a systematic manner. Presently, origami is taught hundreds of different ways, making it difficult and confusing for enthusiasts to advance.

This is where the Taro's Origami Method comes into play. Like martial arts, this method relies on progression through demonstration. Each "kyu" (or level) of the Taro's Origami Method has a different color, similar to how Karate uses a kyu system to award different colored belts at each level.

We have classified these basic folds according to difficulty. This way any student can logically and gradually advance to more complex models once the have mastered all the folds in their current level.

This system excels in helping students understand and identify the folds in each model. Too often, origami is tackled one model at a time, instead of recognizing the similarities between them. Through our teaching method as skills develop, folders will be able to spot the individual folds and patterns in origami and someday begin designing their own models.

The key to quality origami lies not in speed, but in the accuracy of the basics, and by using the Taro's Origami Method any folder can study those basic folds and begin the journey to becoming an origami master!

6th Kyu Yellow Belt

Diagonal Fold

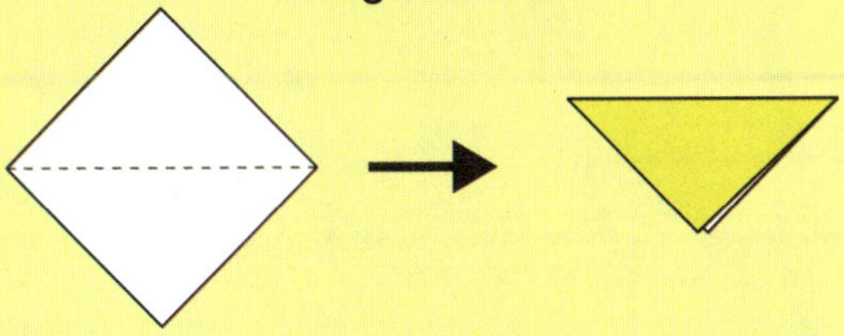

Book Fold

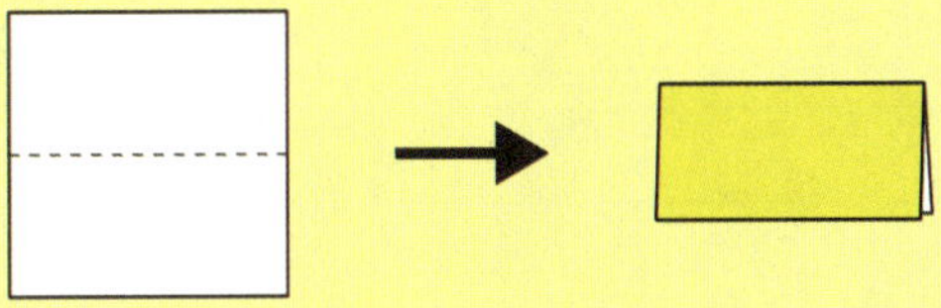

Kite Fold/Base

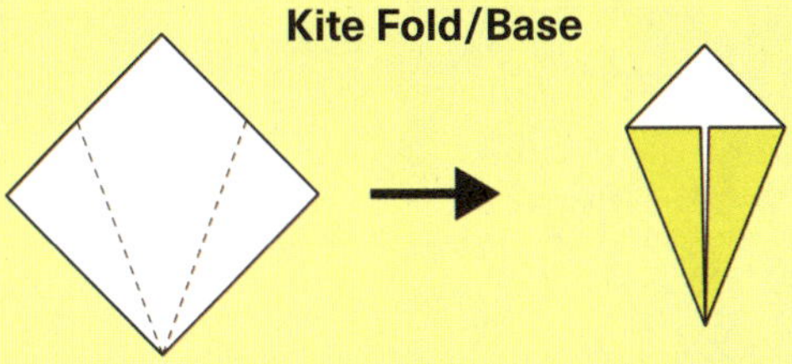

Blintz Fold/Base

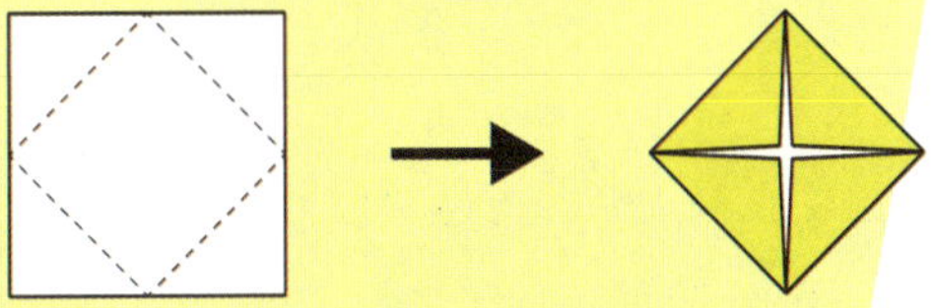

Cabinet Fold/Base

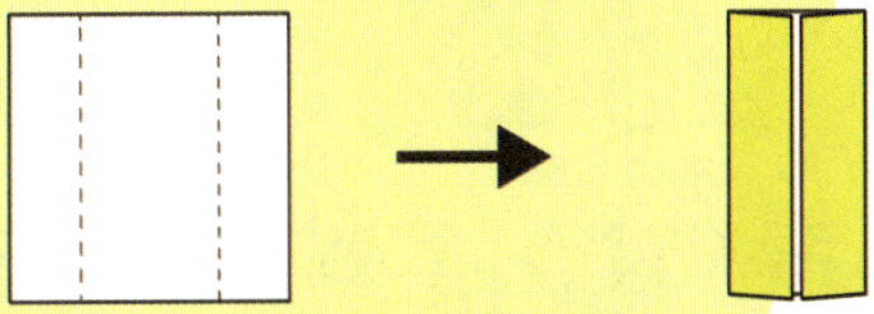

Square Base

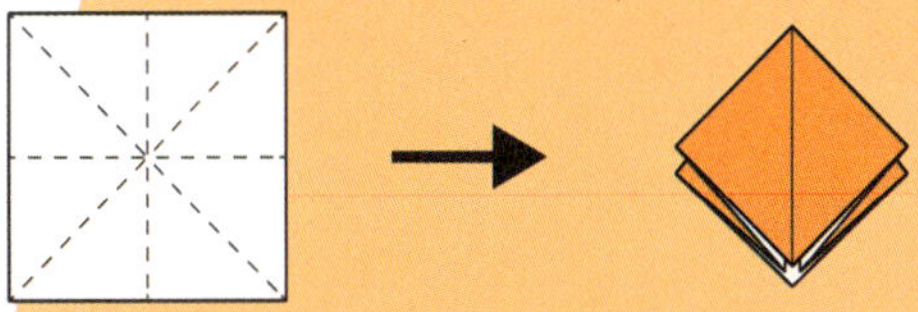

Squash Fold

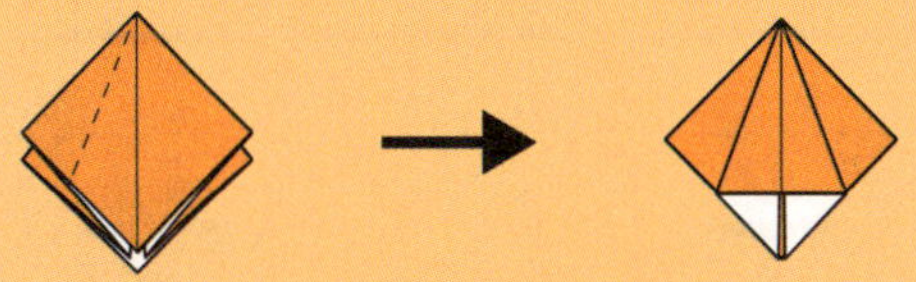

Pleat Fold

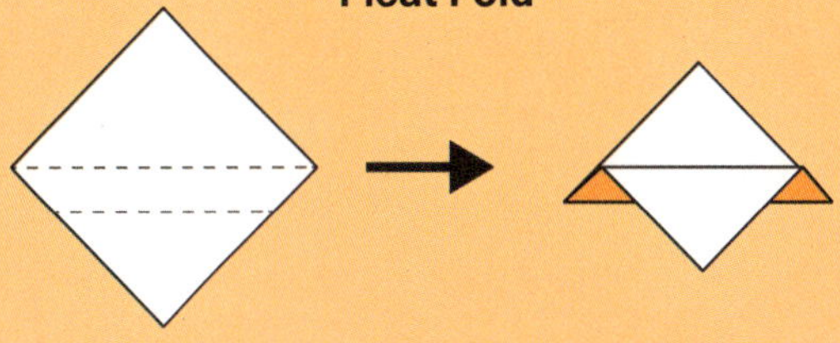

Waterbomb Base

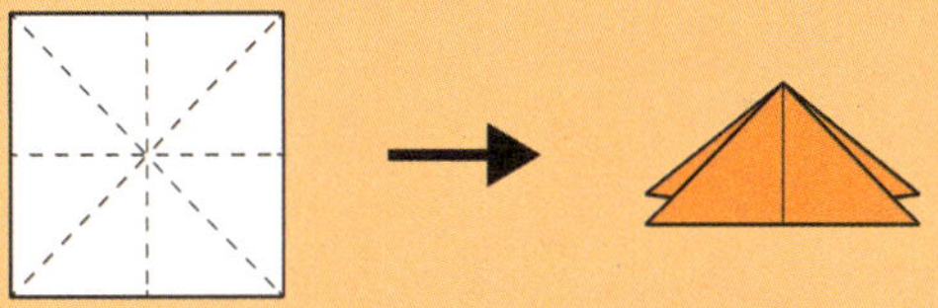

Rabbit-ear Fold

5th Kyu Orange Belt

4th Kyu Blue Belt

Petal Fold

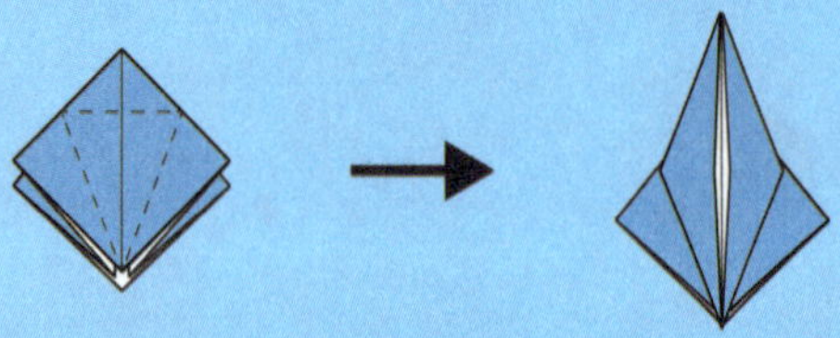

Bird Base

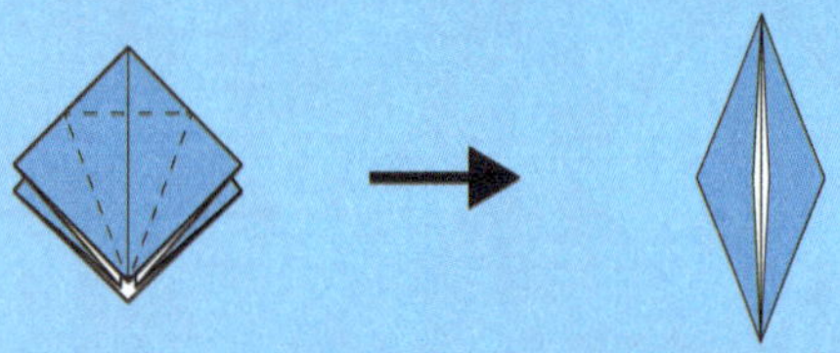

Fish Base

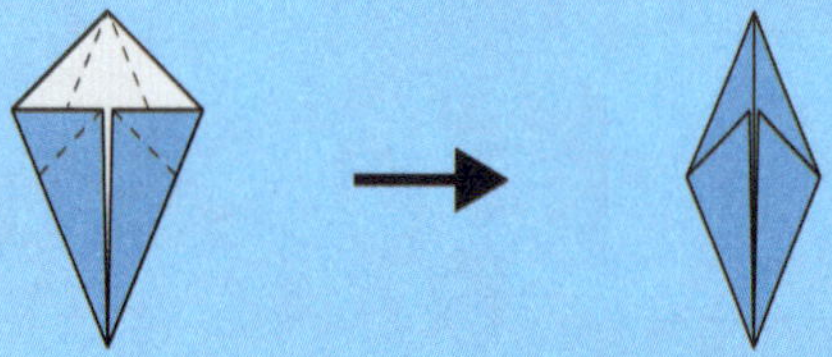

Double Boat Base

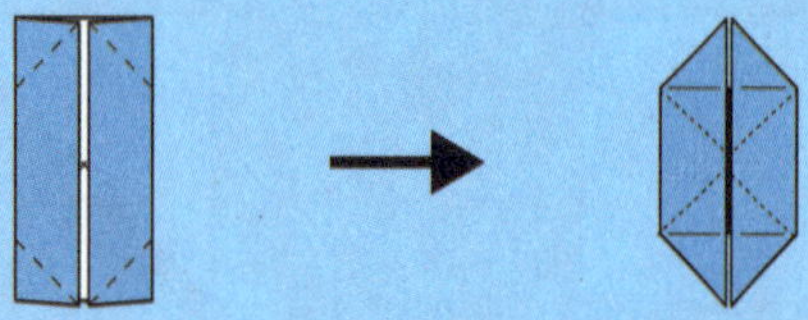

Inside Reverse Fold

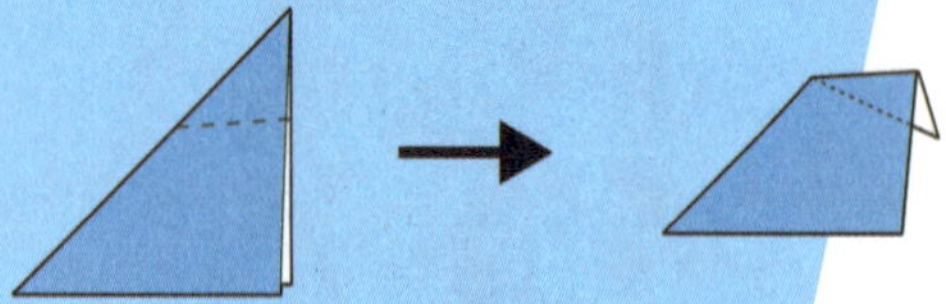

3rd Kyu Purple Belt

Pinwheel Base

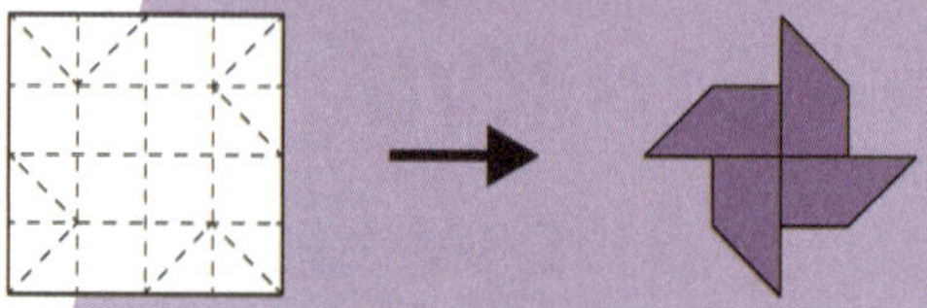

Outside Reverse Fold

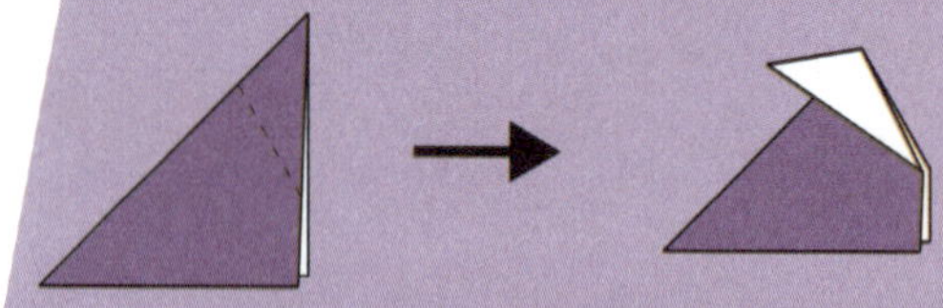

Fox Fold

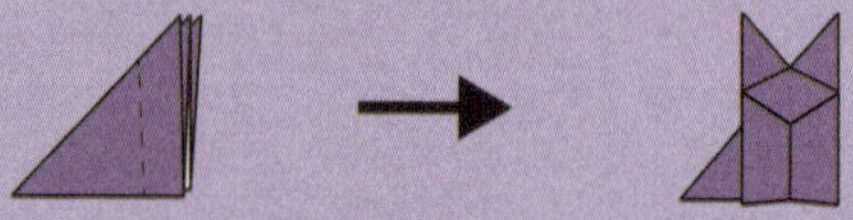

Flower Base

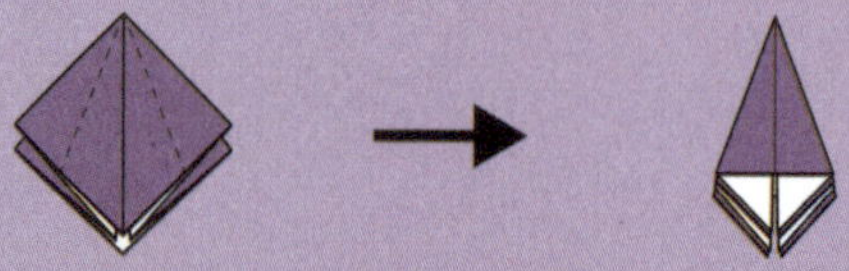

Frog Base

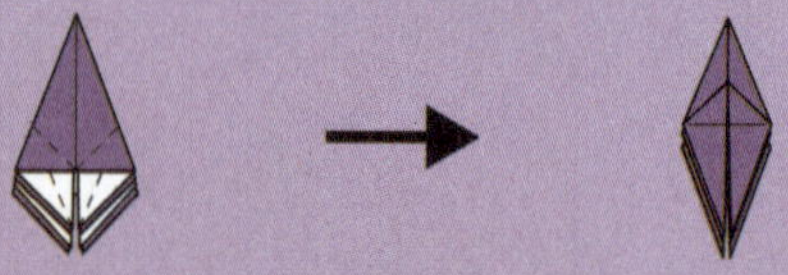

2nd Kyu
Green Belt

Yakko-san Base

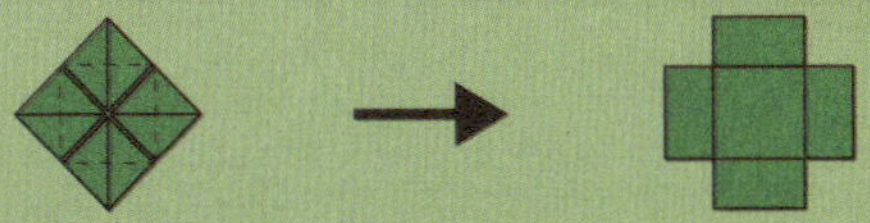

Open Sink Fold

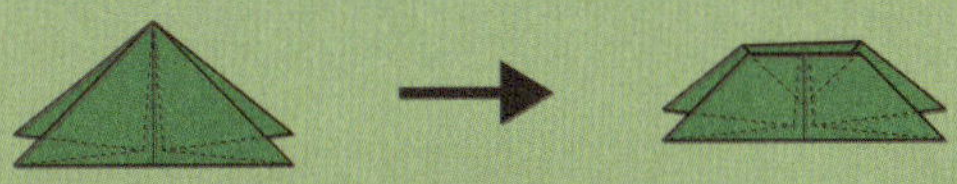

Closed Sink Fold

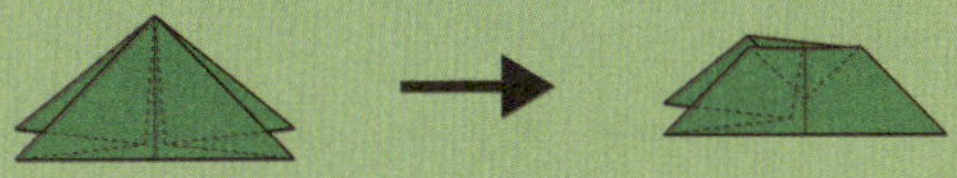

Outside Crimp Fold

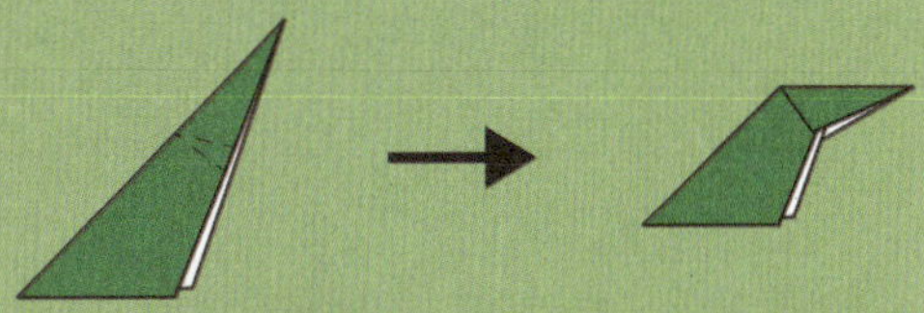

Inside Crimp Fold

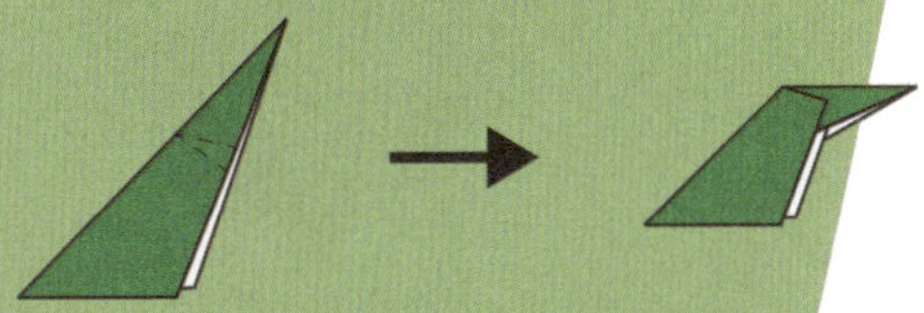

Swivel Fold

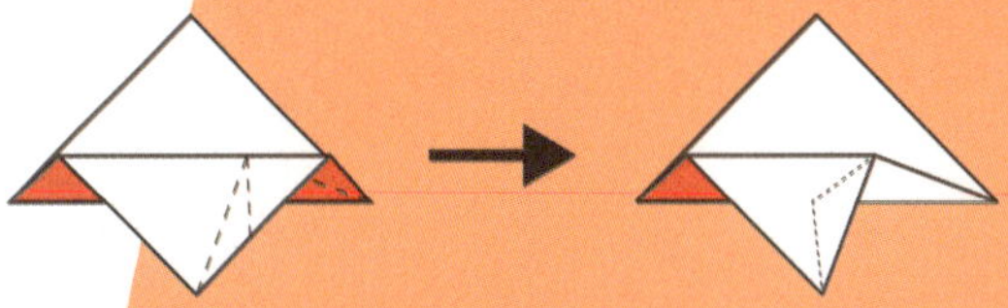

Double Open Sink Fold

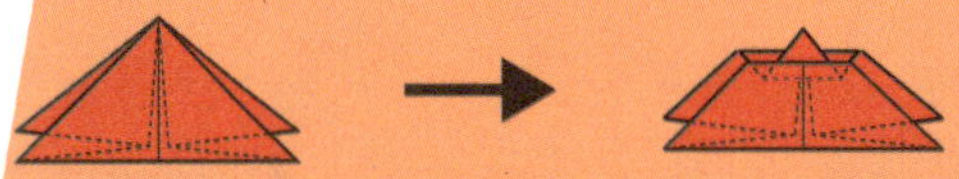

Double Closed Sink Fold

Double Reverse Fold

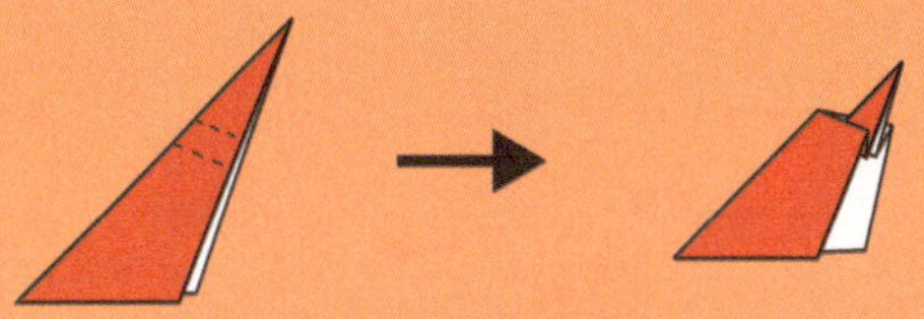

Double Rabbit-ear Fold

1st Kyu
Red Belt

Samurai Helmet

● Diagonal Fold

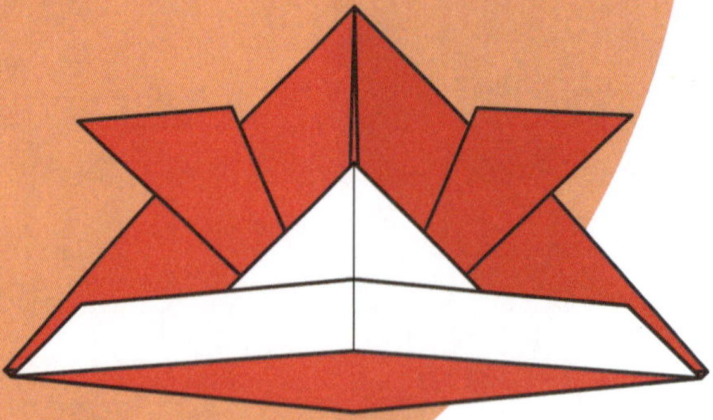

1

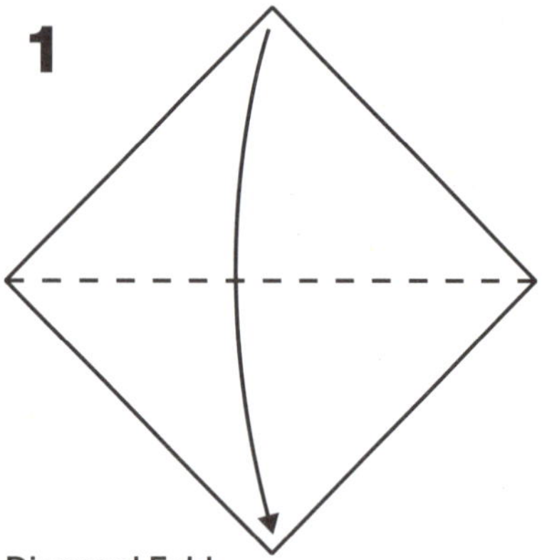

Diagonal Fold

2

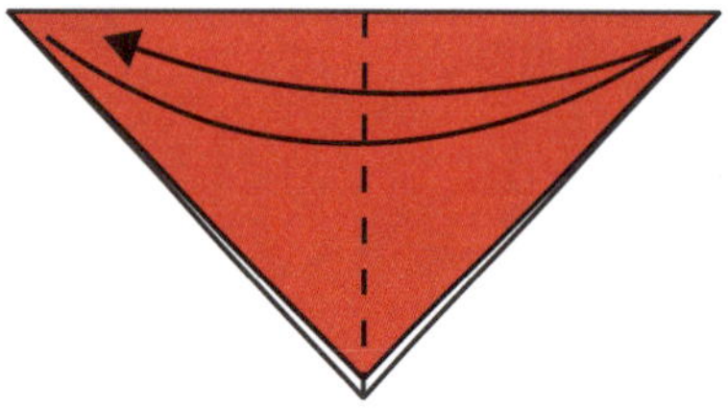

Fold and unfold

3

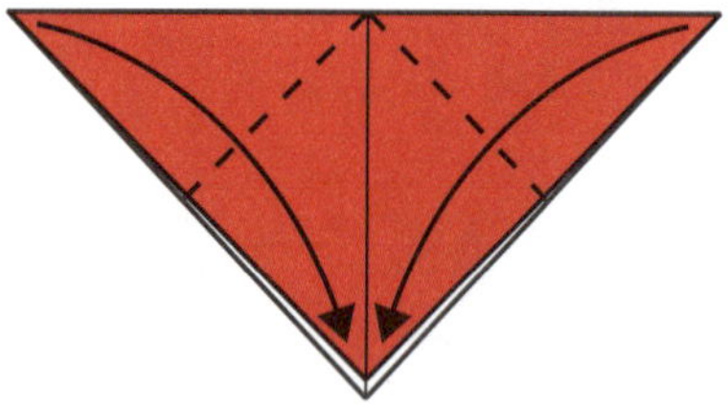

4

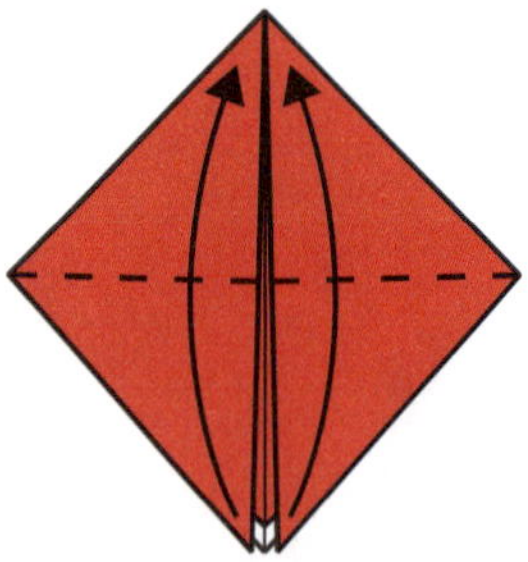

5

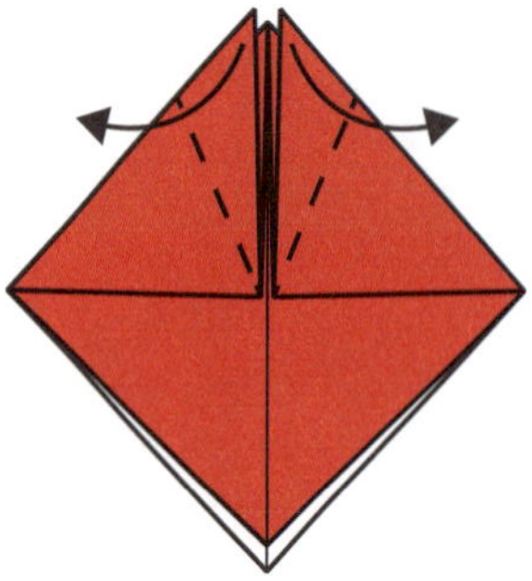

6

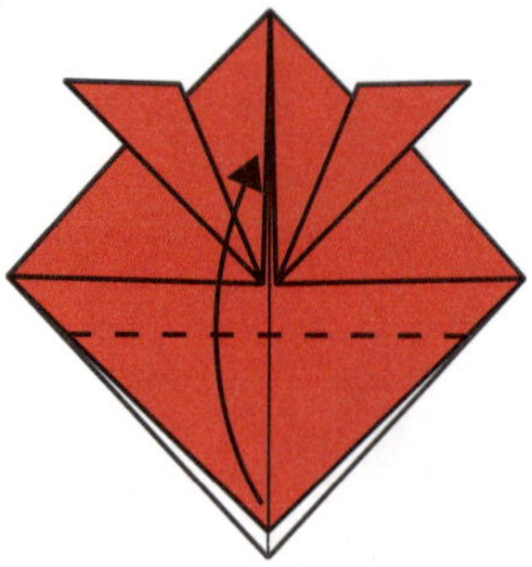

Fold top flap up

7

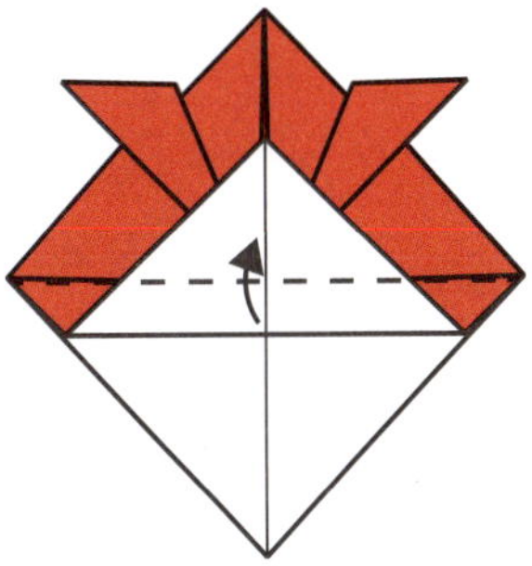

8

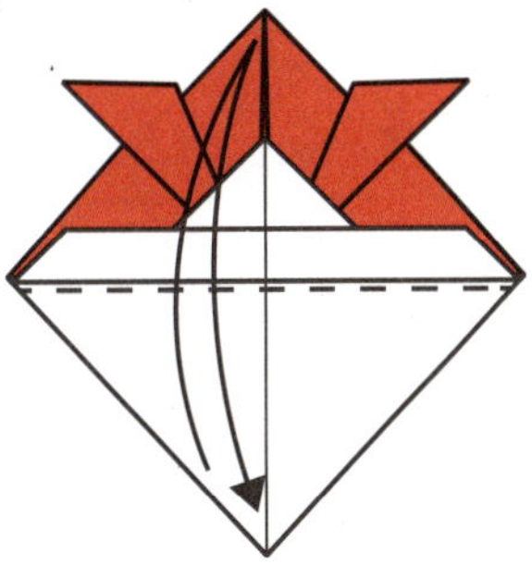

Fold and unfold

9

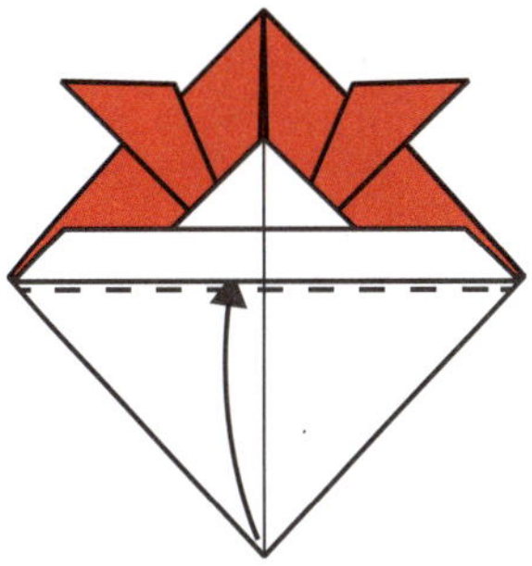

Tuck inside

10

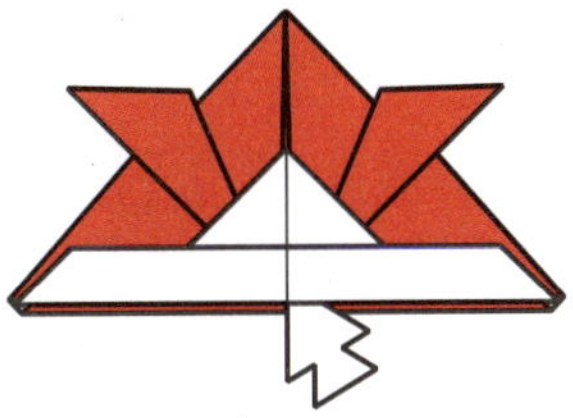

Open

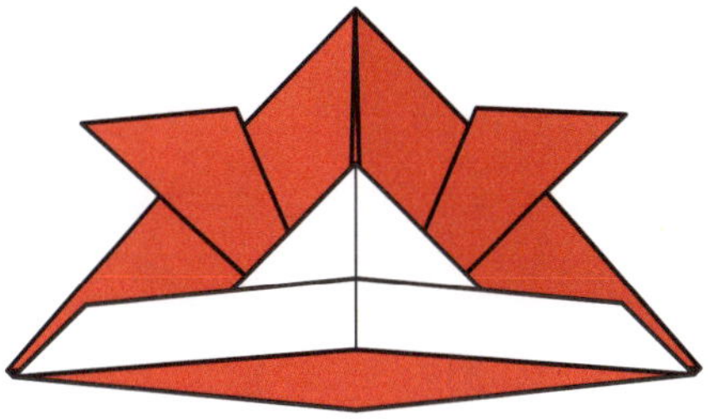

Samurai Helmet

Sun(flower)

- Book Fold
- Blintz Fold

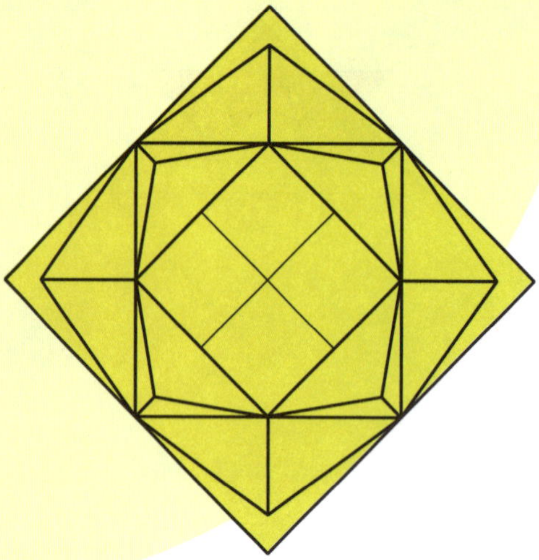

1

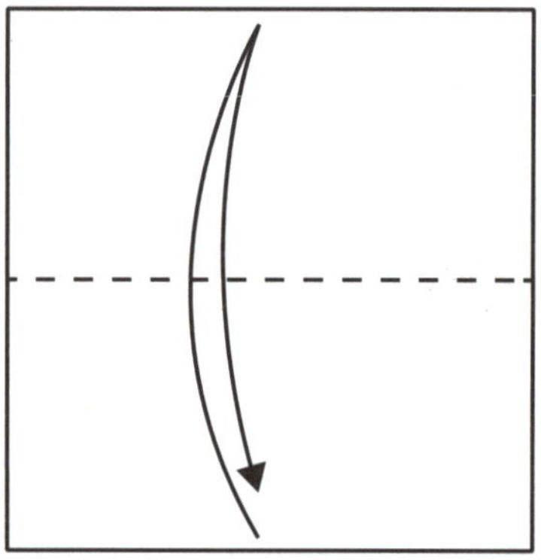

Book fold and unfold

2

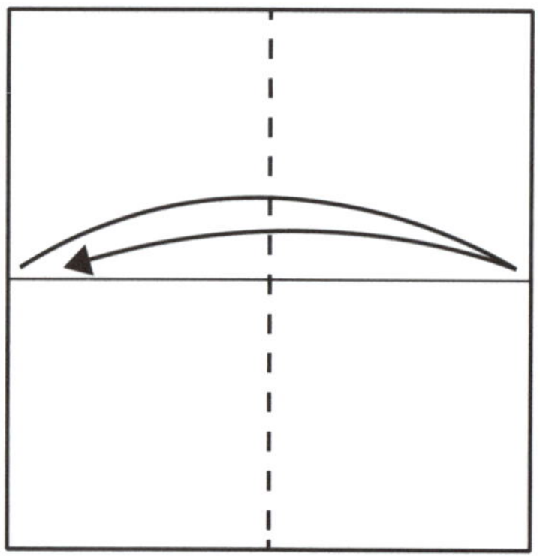

3

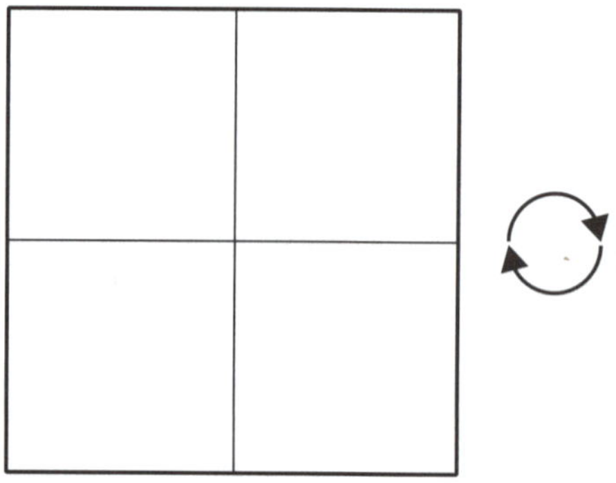

Rotate

4

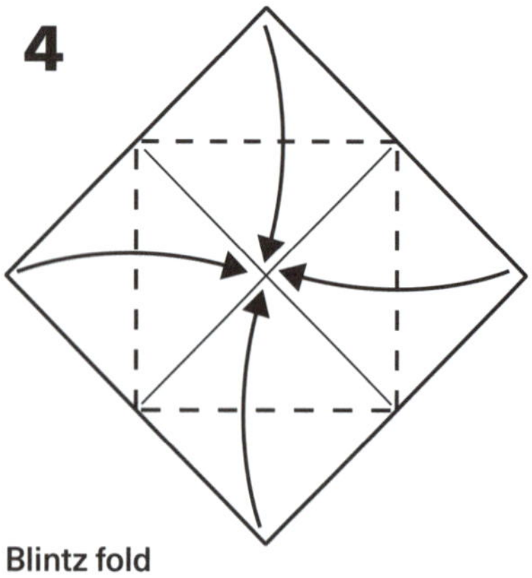

Blintz fold

5

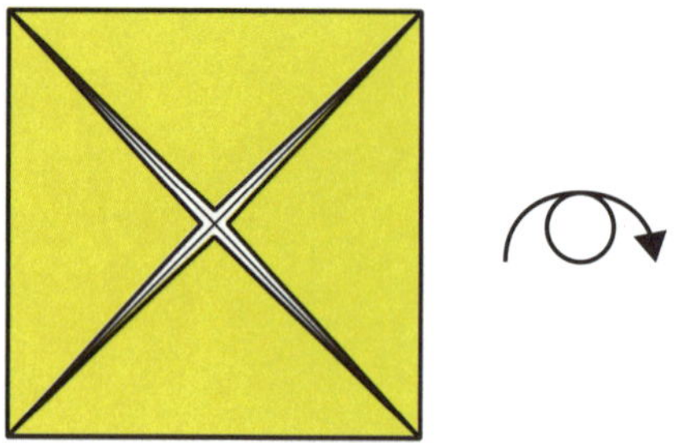

Turn over

6

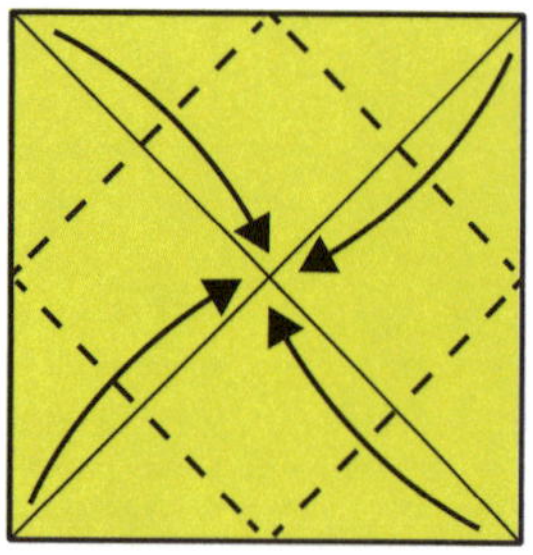

Blintz fold

7

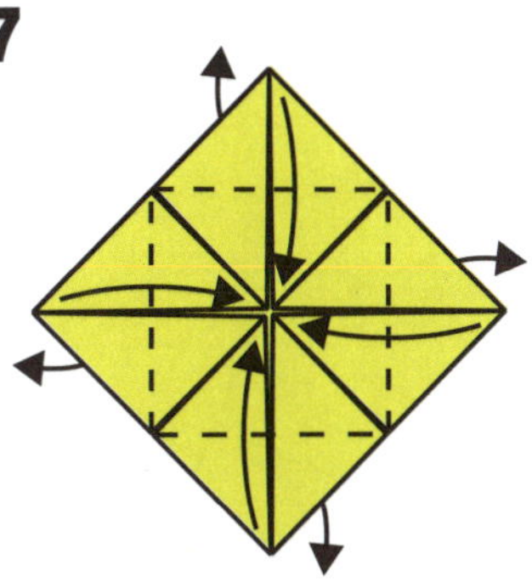

Blintz fold again, and let the flaps behind out

8

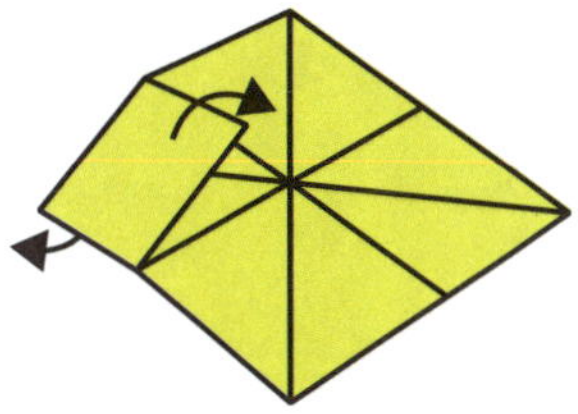

3D step in progress

9

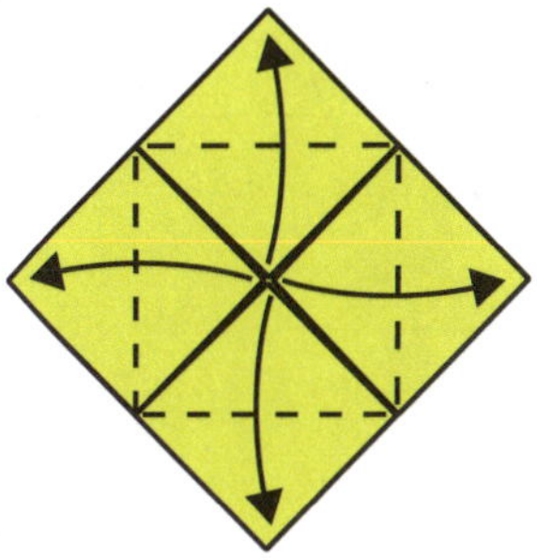

10

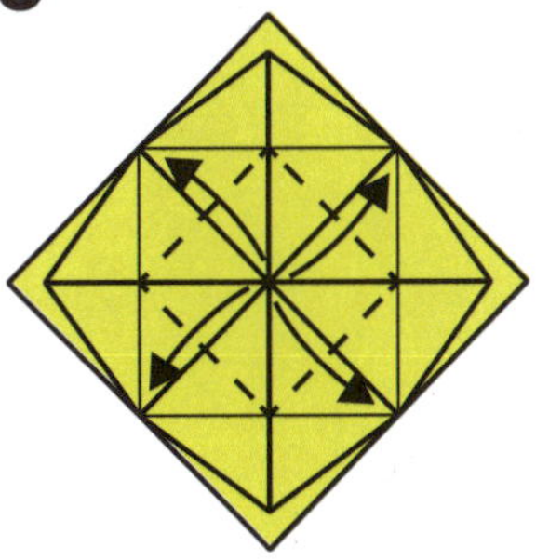

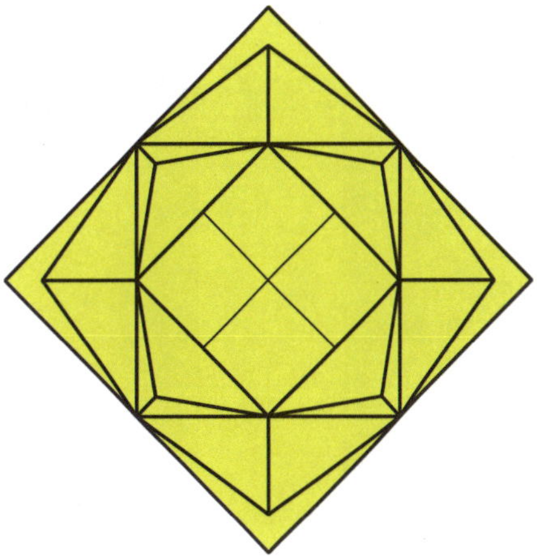

Sun(flower)

Crescent Moon

- Book Fold
- Diagonal Fold
- Blintz Fold
- Cabinet Fold

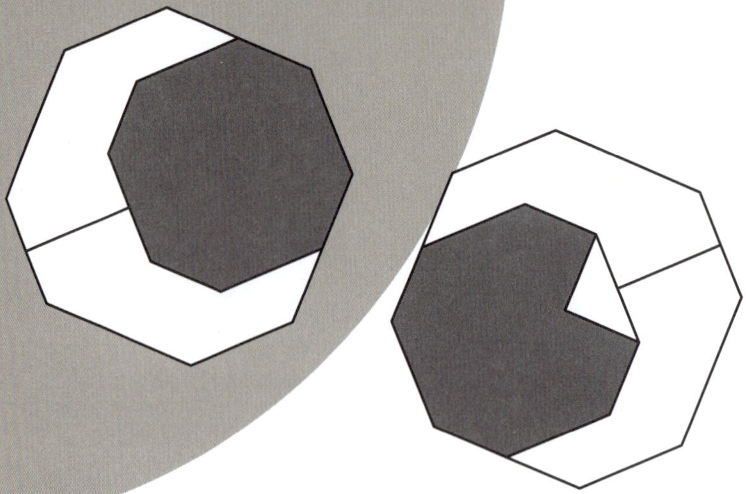

1

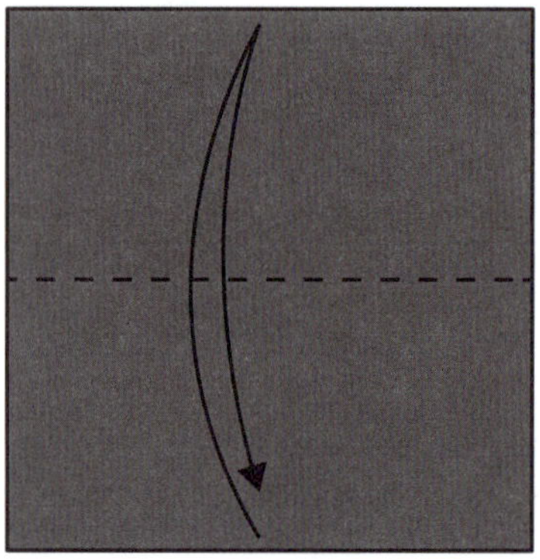

Book fold and unfold

2

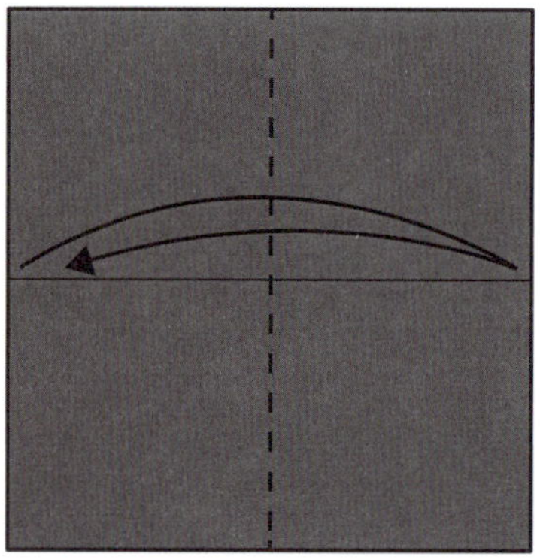

3

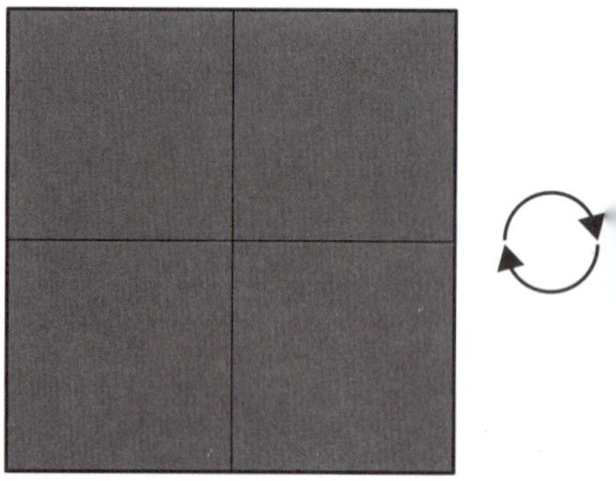

Rotate

4

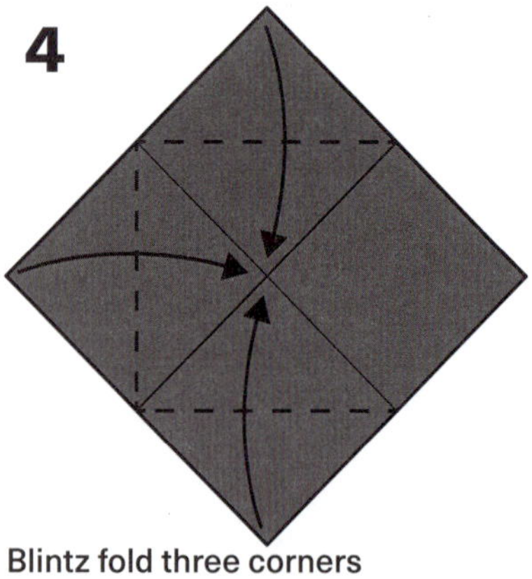

Blintz fold three corners

5

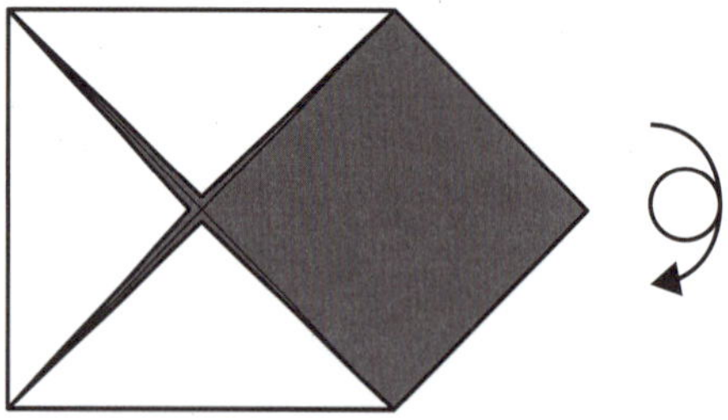

Turn over

6

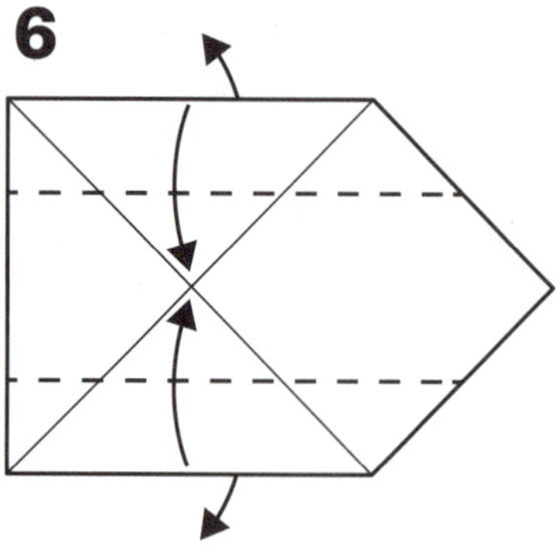

Cabinet fold, and bring hidden flaps out

7

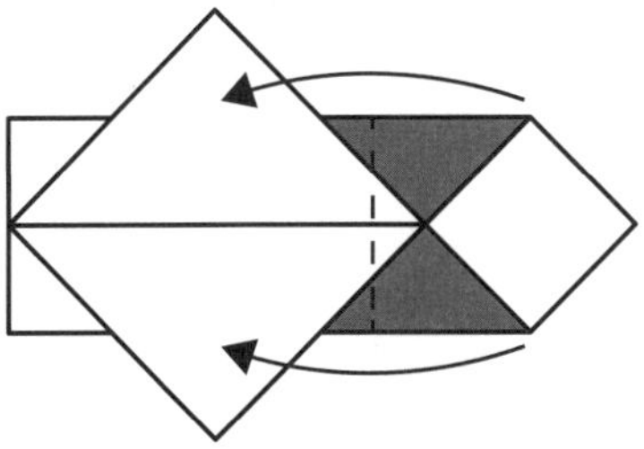

8

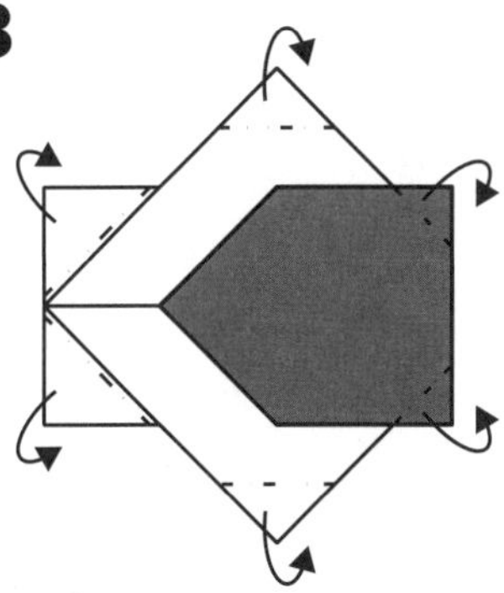

9

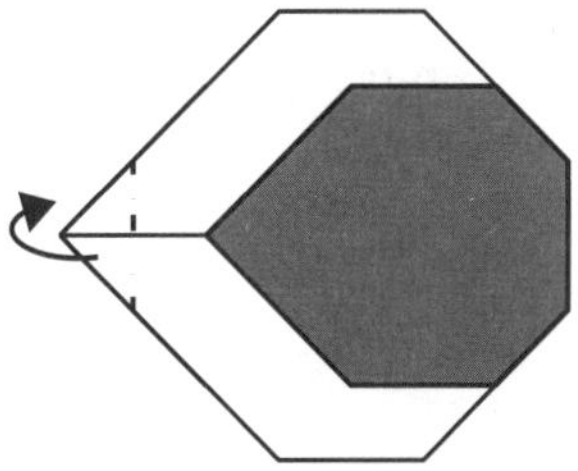

10

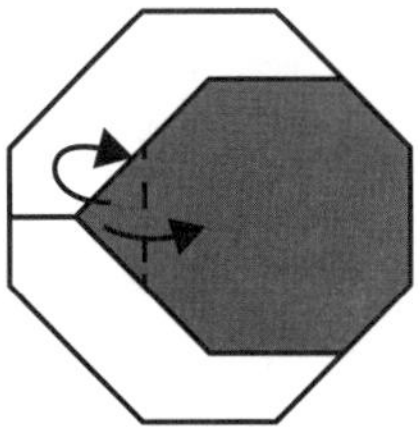

Fold forward or behind for two different moons

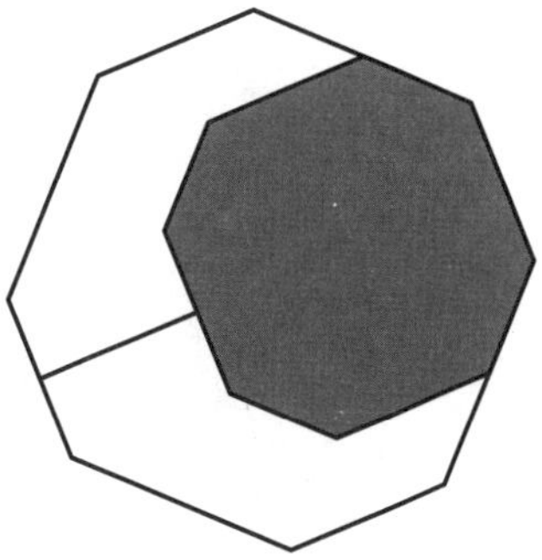

Crescent Moon

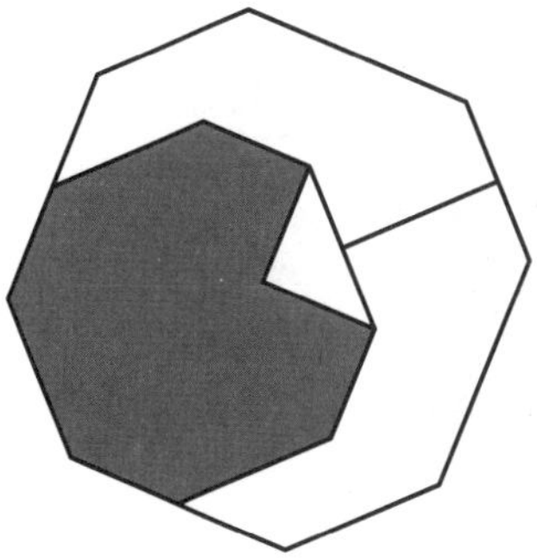

Man in the Moon

Garden Gnome

- Diagonal Fold
- Kite Fold
- Cabinet Fold
- Blintz Fold
- Pleat Fold

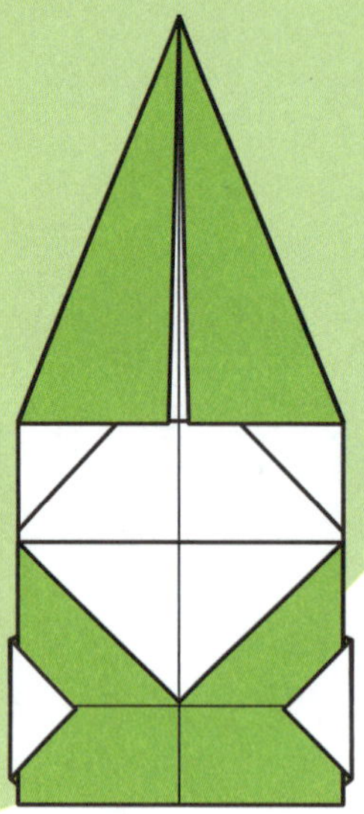

1

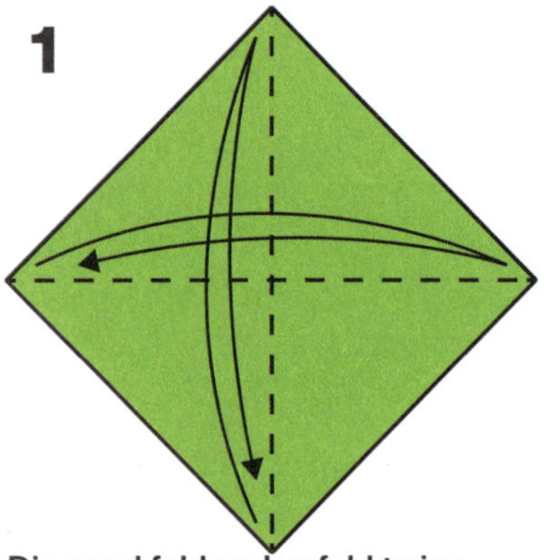

Diagonal fold and unfold twice

2

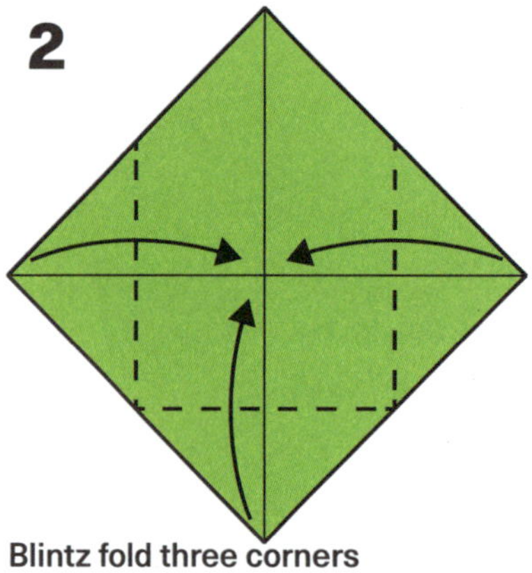

Blintz fold three corners

3

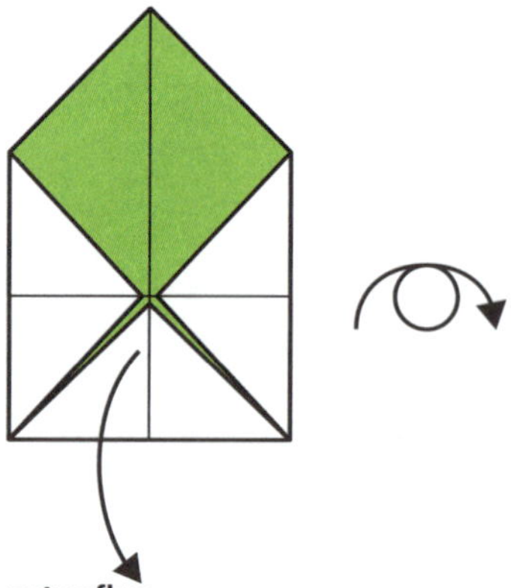

Unfold center flap
Turn over

4

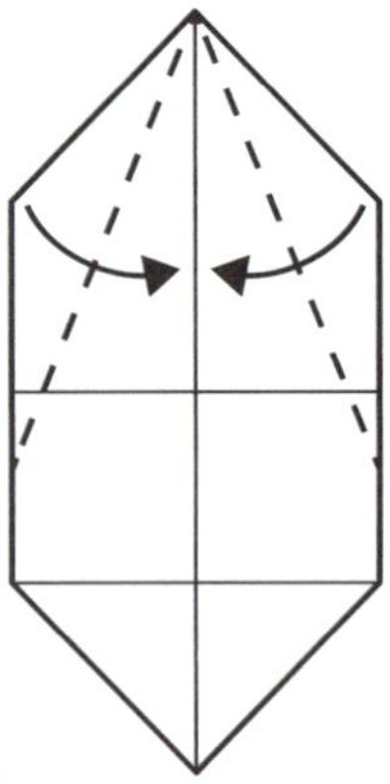

Kite fold

5

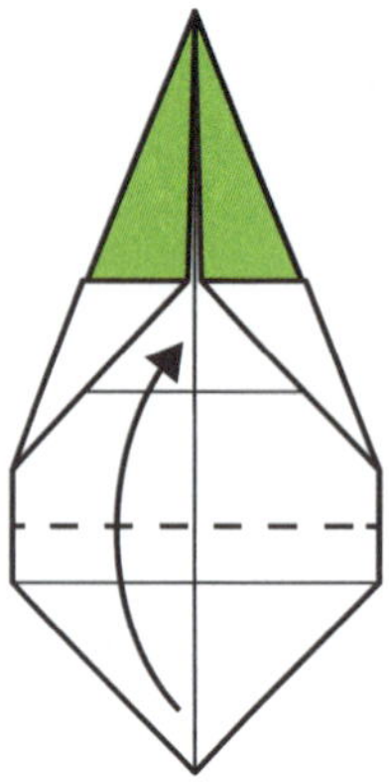

6

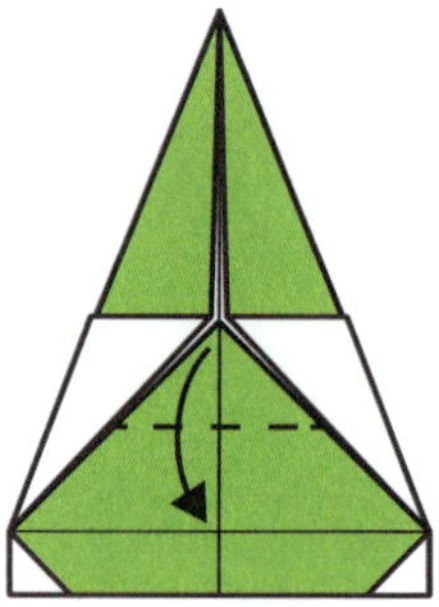

7

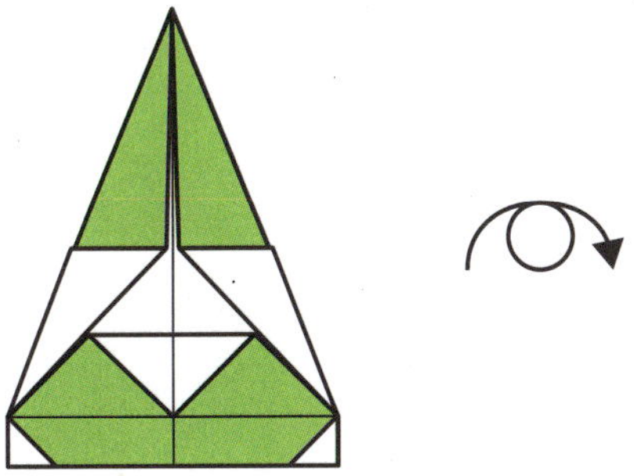

8

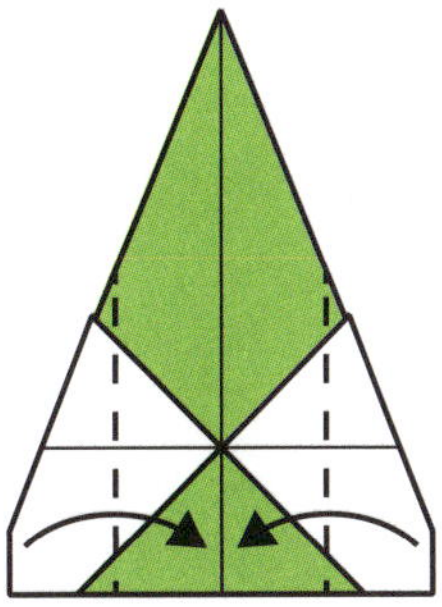

Cabinet fold

9

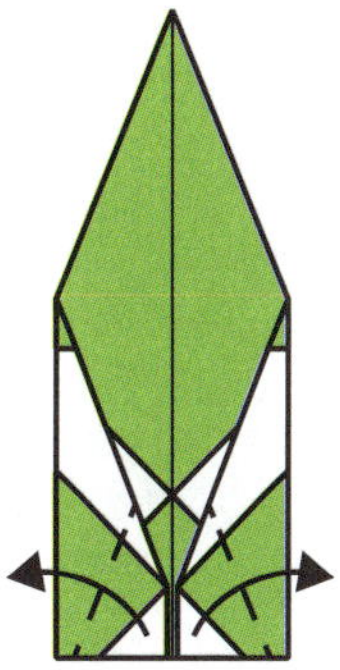

10

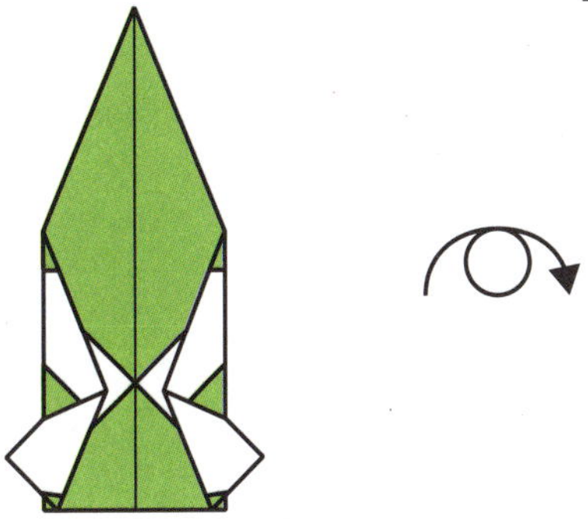

Turn over

11

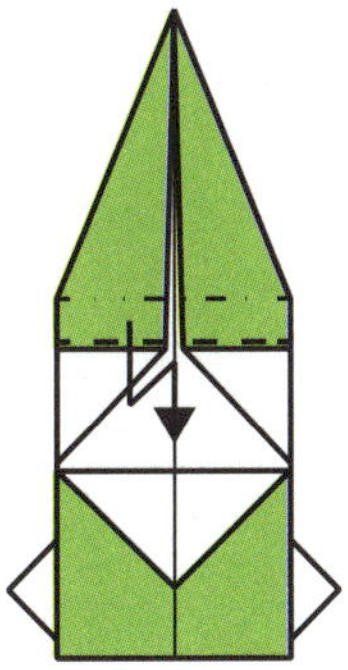

Pleat Fold

12

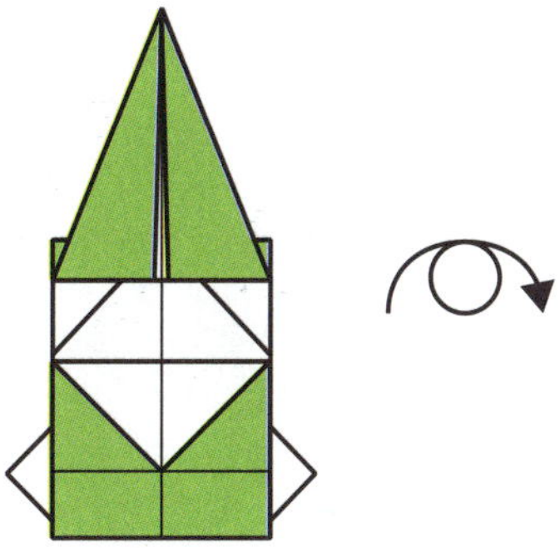

Turn over

13

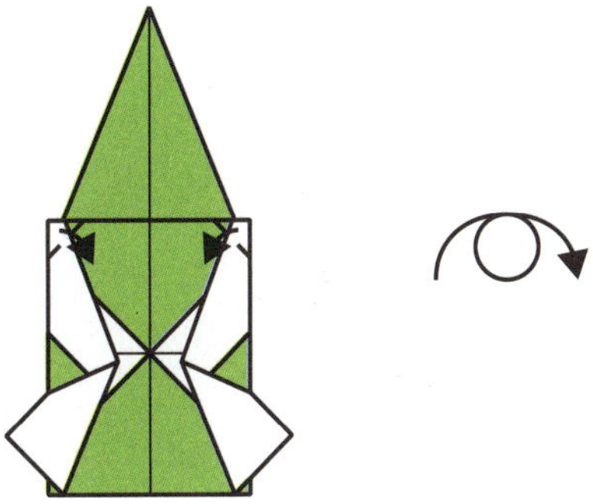

Fold two corners
Turn over

14

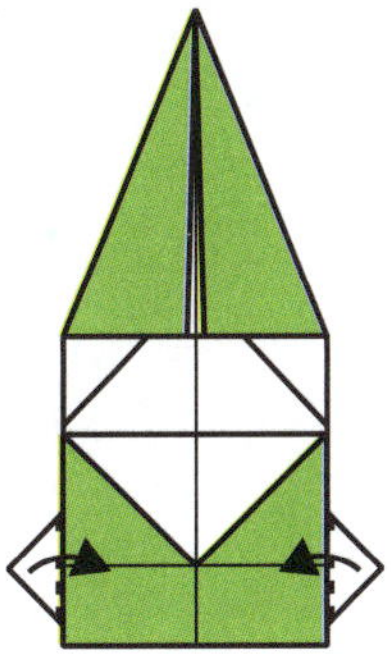

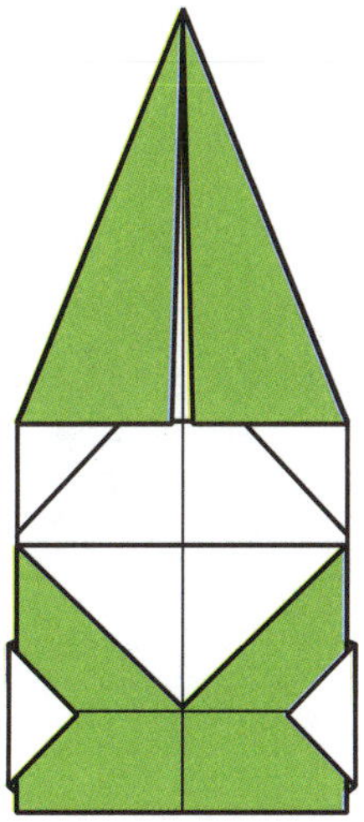

Garden Gnome

Sailboat

- Diagonal Fold
- Book Fold
- Pleat Fold
- Square Base

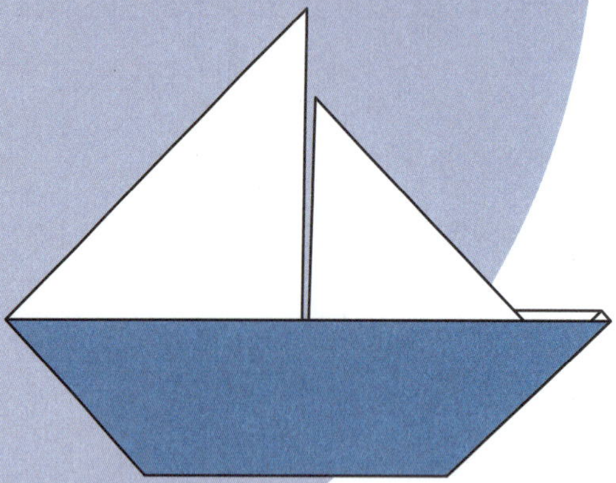

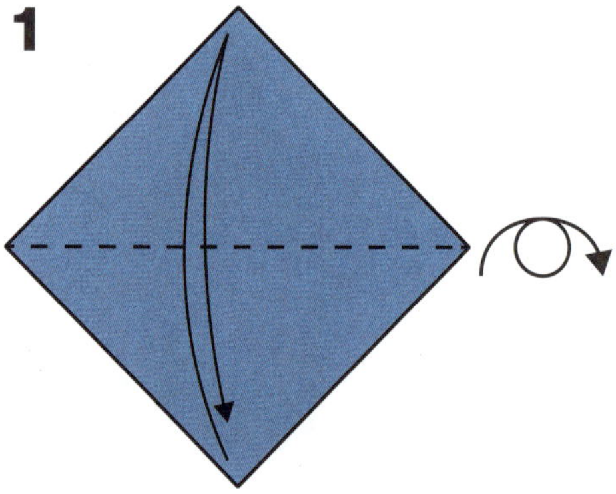

1 Diagonal fold and unfold
Turn over

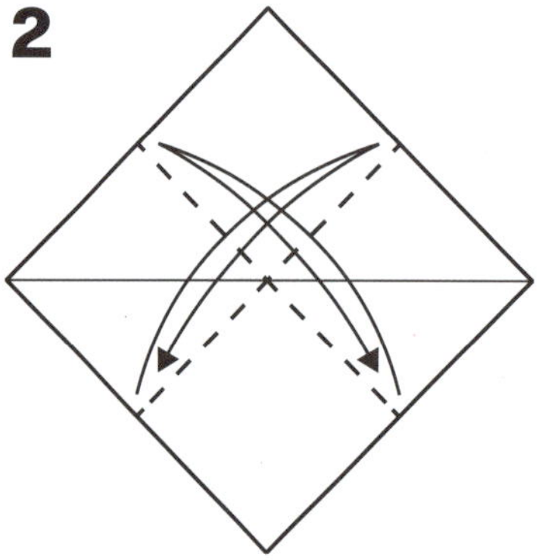

2 Book fold and unfold twice

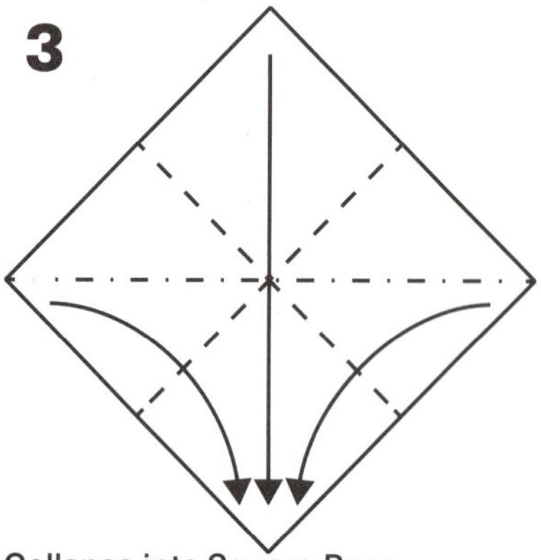

3 Collapse into Square Base

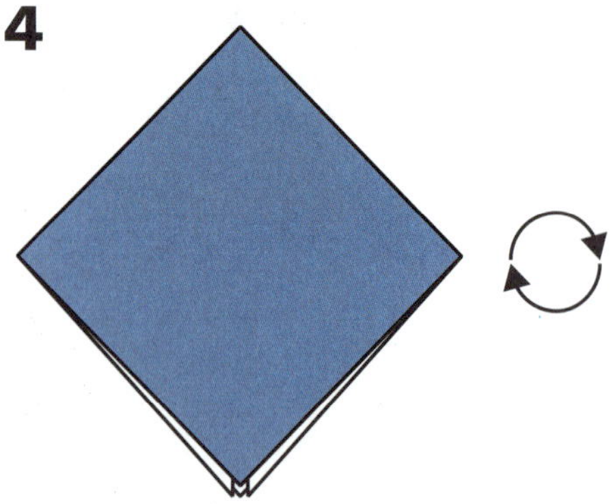

4 Rotate

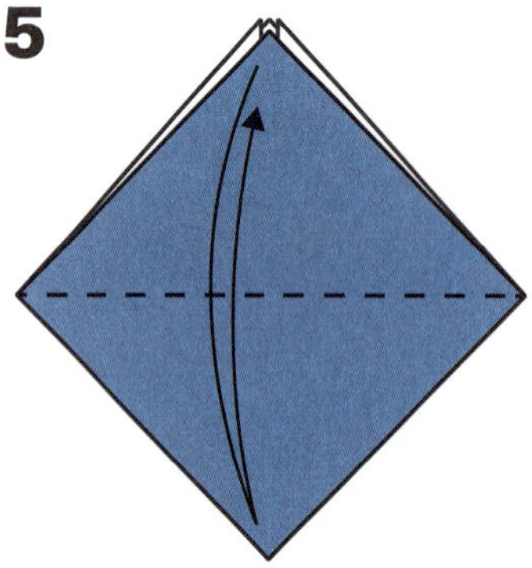

5 Fold and unfold
Repeat behind

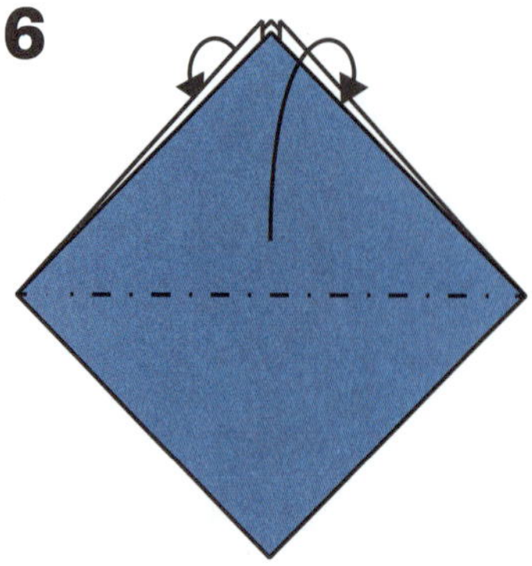

6 Tuck inside
Repeat behind

7

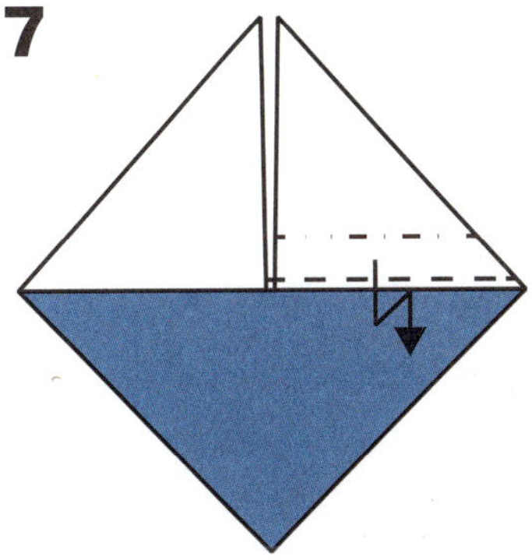

Pleat fold

8

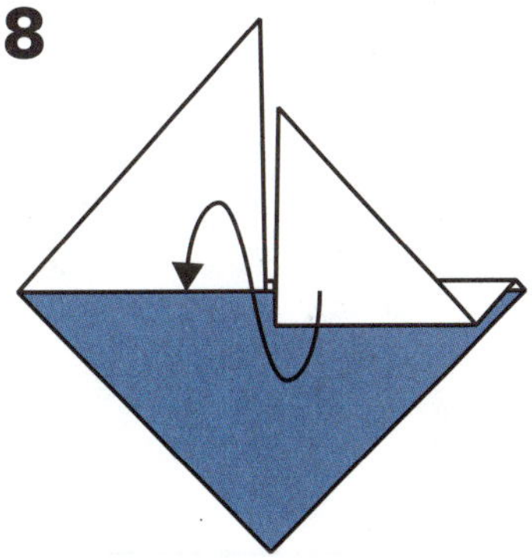

Tuck inside

9

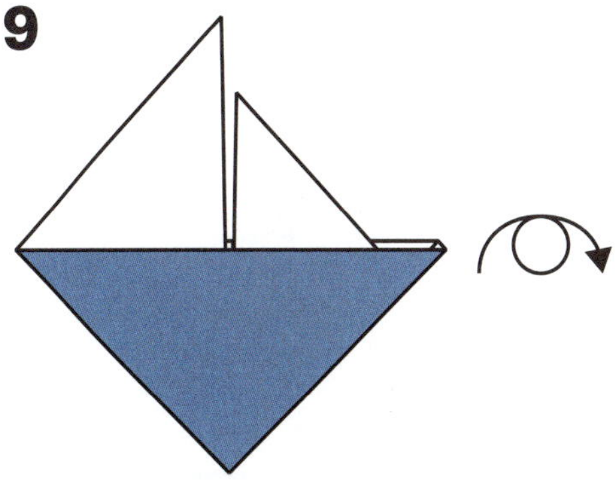

Turn over

10

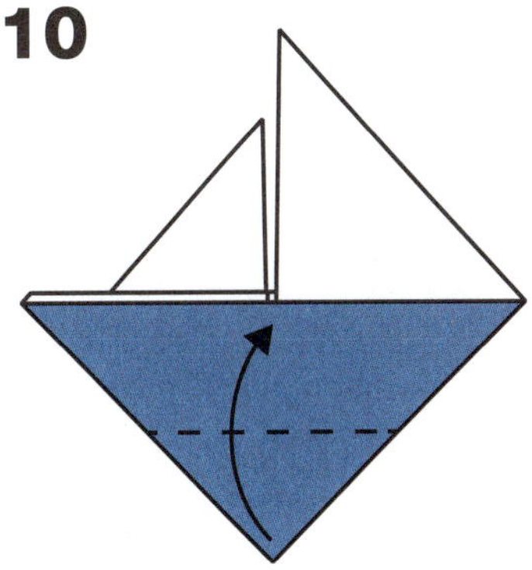

Text

11

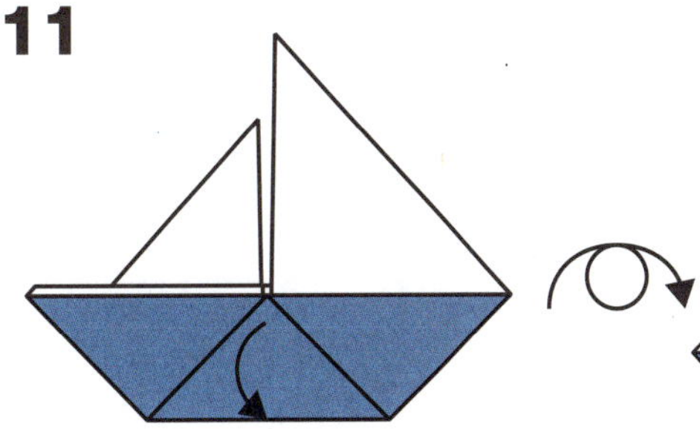

Unfold to make stand
Turn over

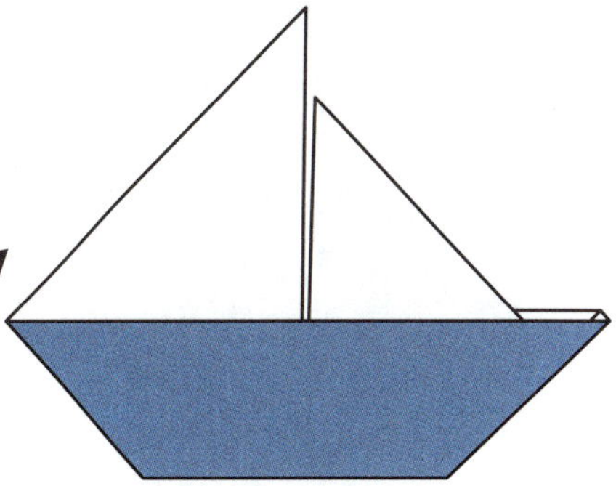

Sailboat

Frog

- Book Fold
- Diagonal Fold
- Kite Fold
- Waterbomb Base

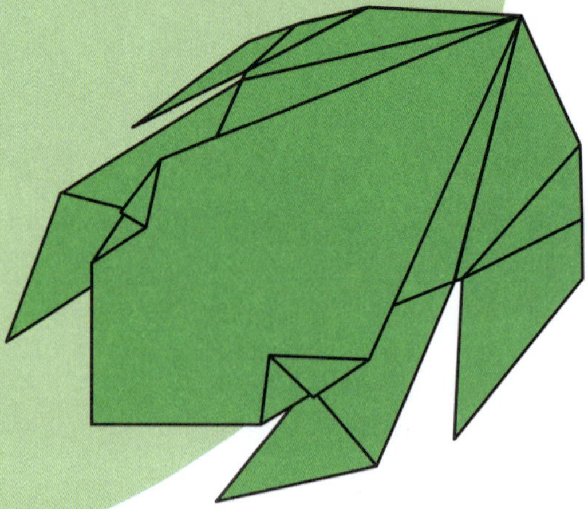

1

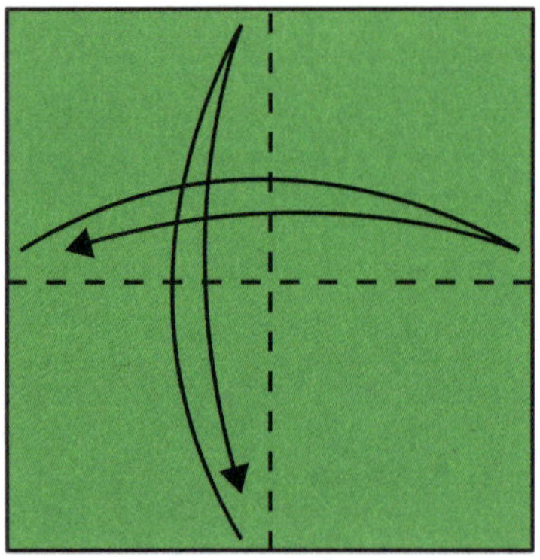

Book fold and unfold twice
Turn over

2

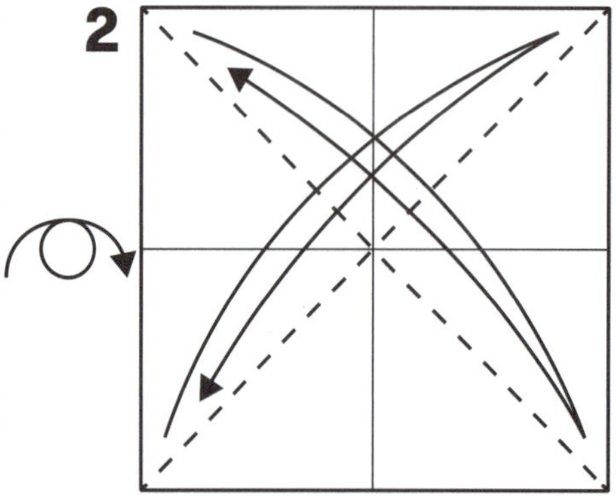

Diagonal fold and unfold twice

3

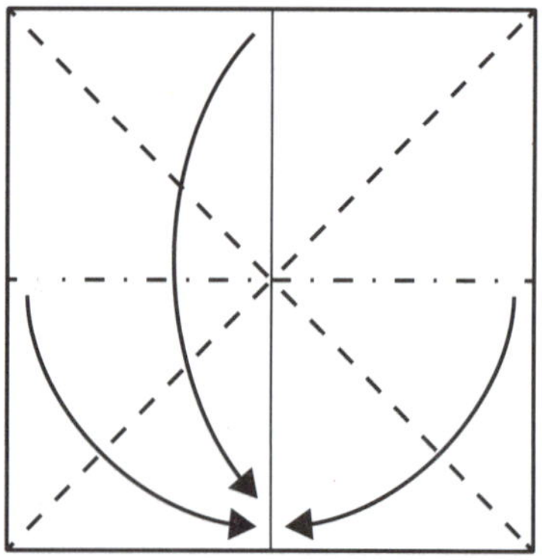

Collapse into Waterbomb Base

4

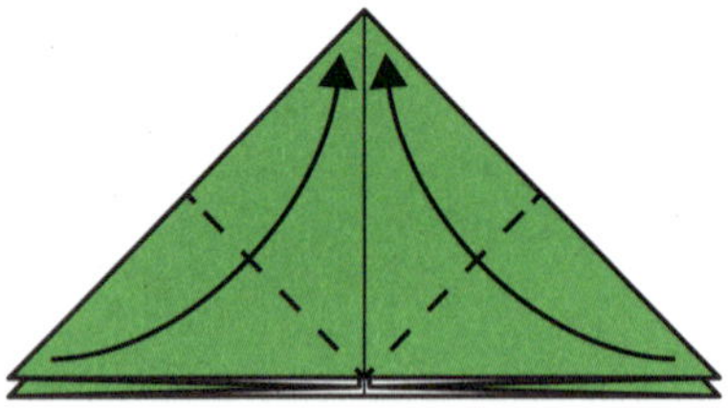

5

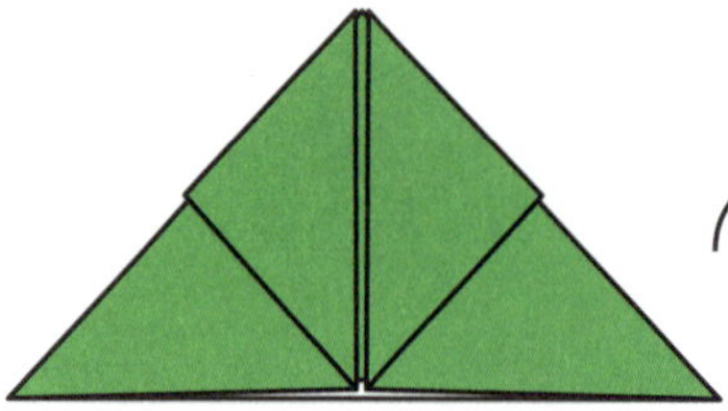

Turn over

6

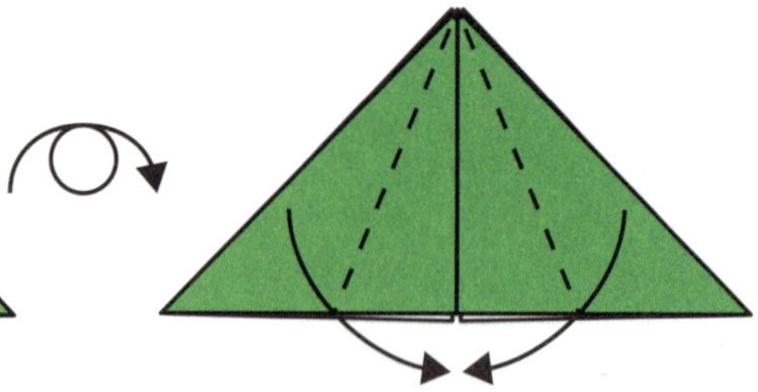

Kite fold

7

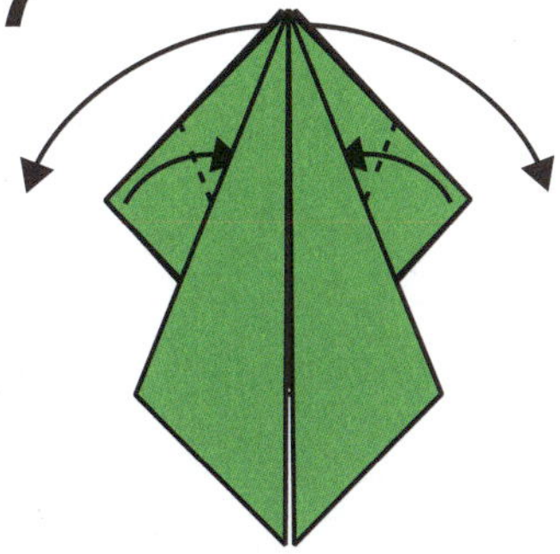

Kite fold under top layers and bring hidden flaps out

8

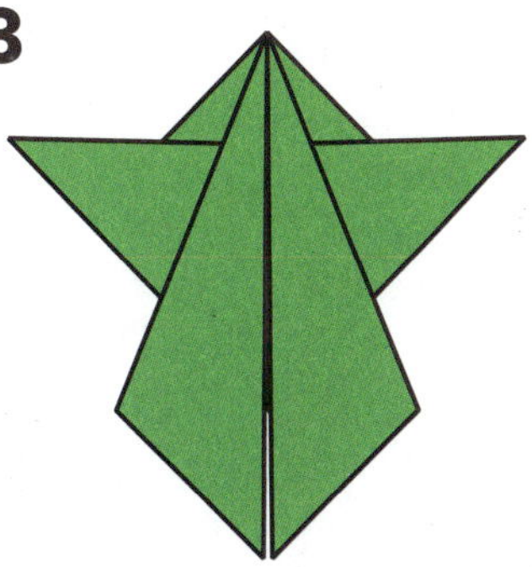

Turn over

9

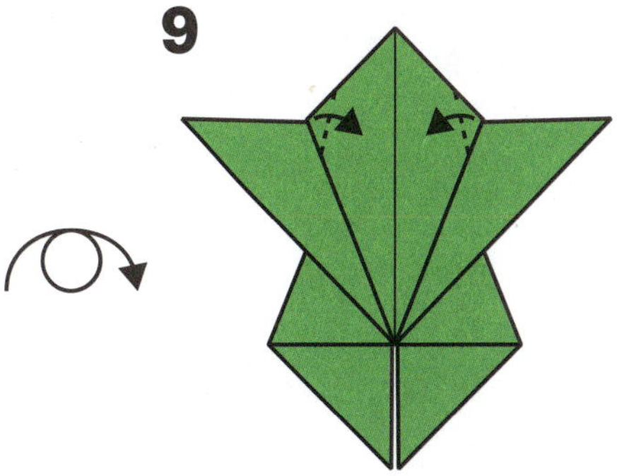

10

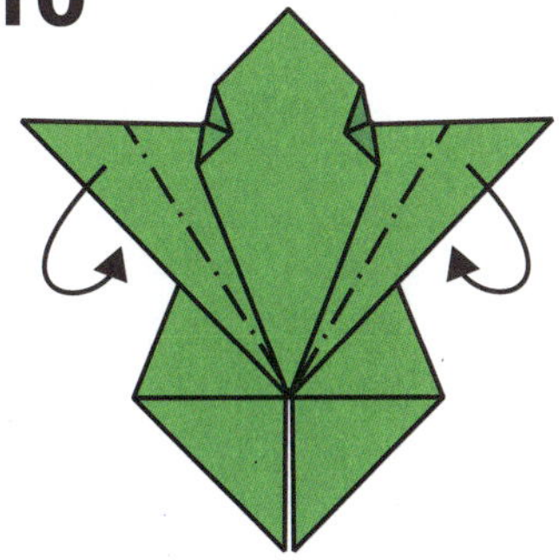

Fold flaps behind

11

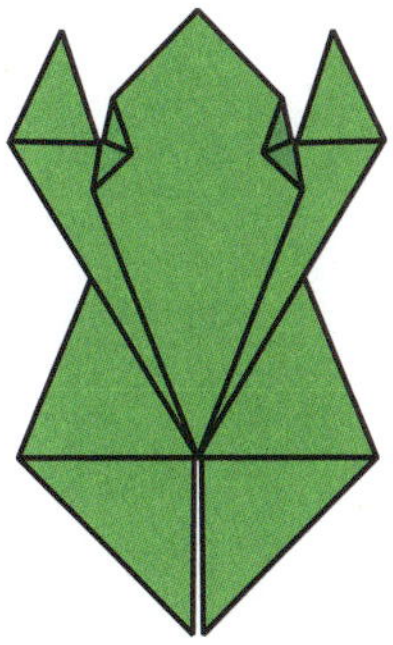

Turn over

12

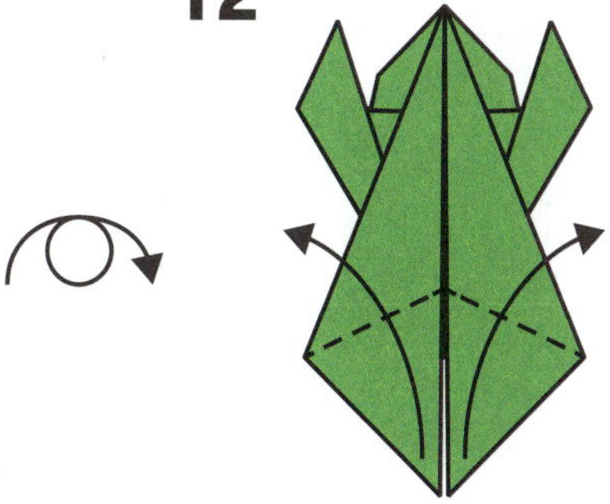

13

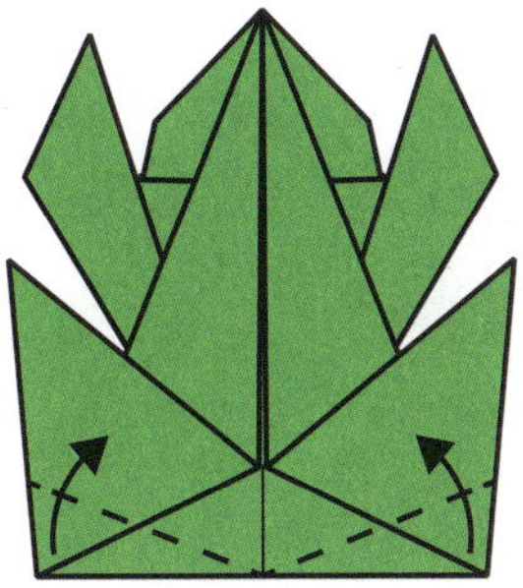

14

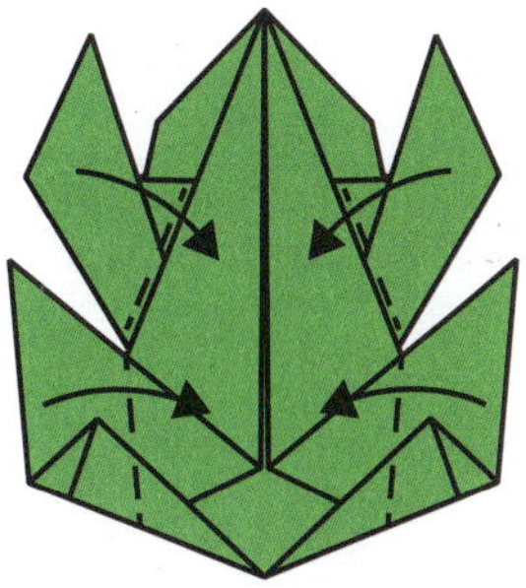

Partially fold in four flaps
Turn over

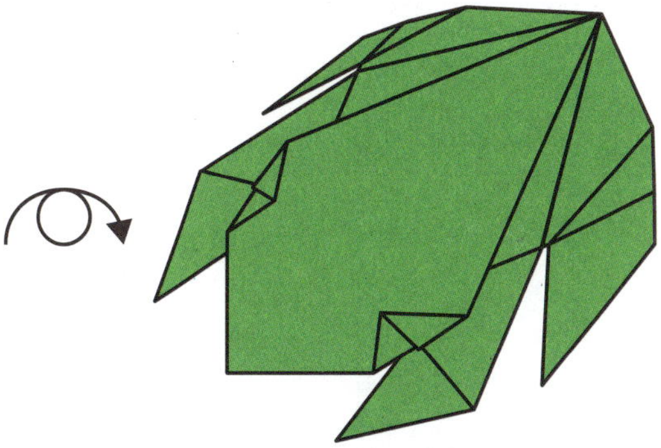

Frog

Mouse

- Diagonal Fold
- Kite Fold
- Pleat Fold
- Rabbit-ear Fold
- Fish Base

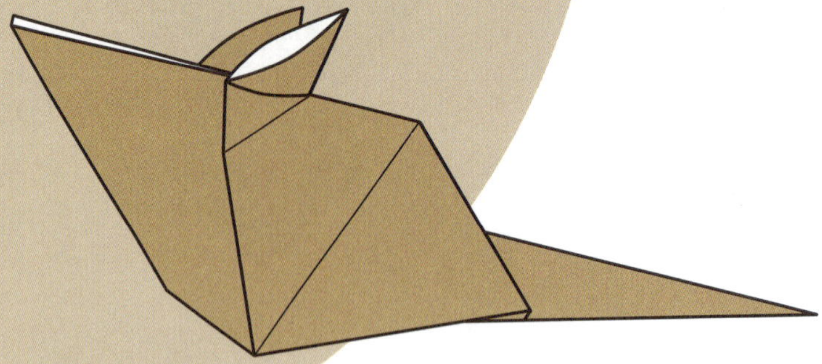

1

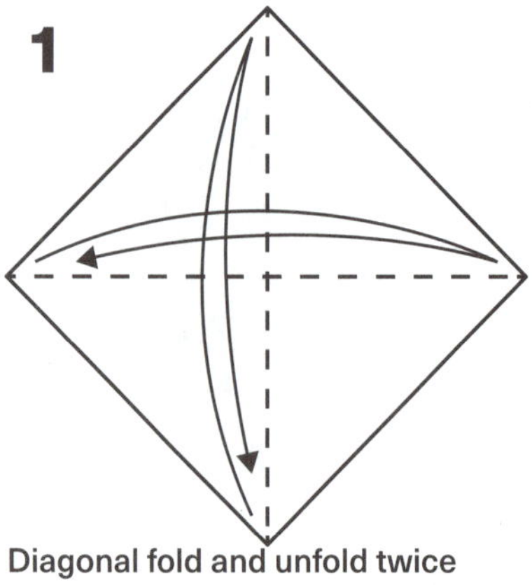

Diagonal fold and unfold twice

2

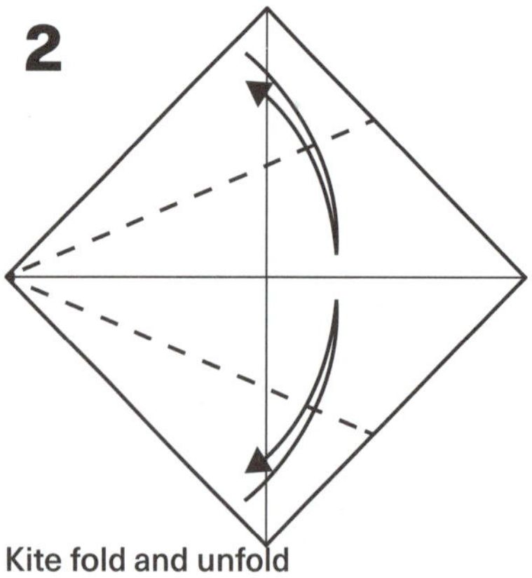

Kite fold and unfold

3

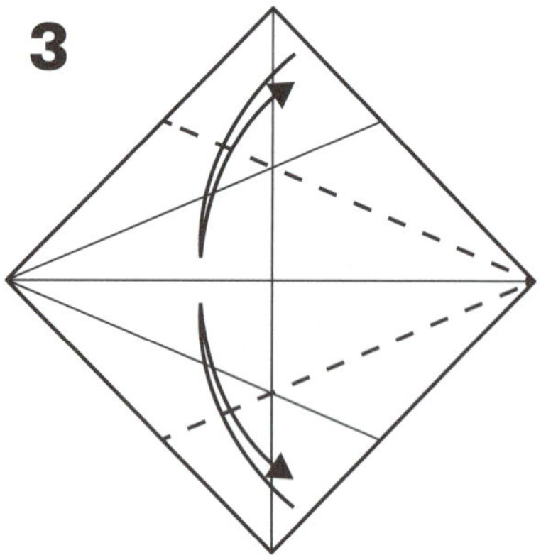

4

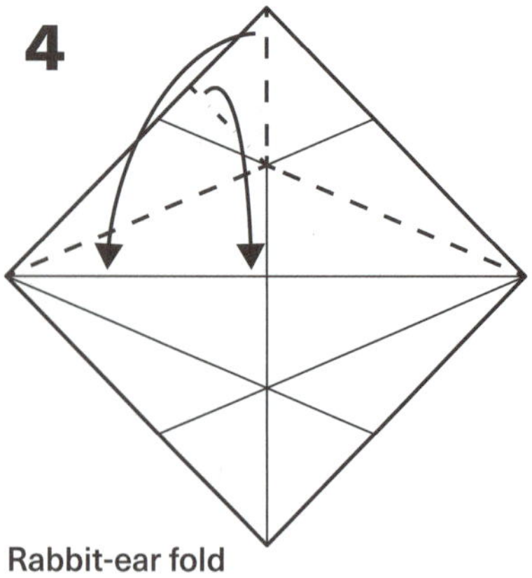

Rabbit-ear fold

5

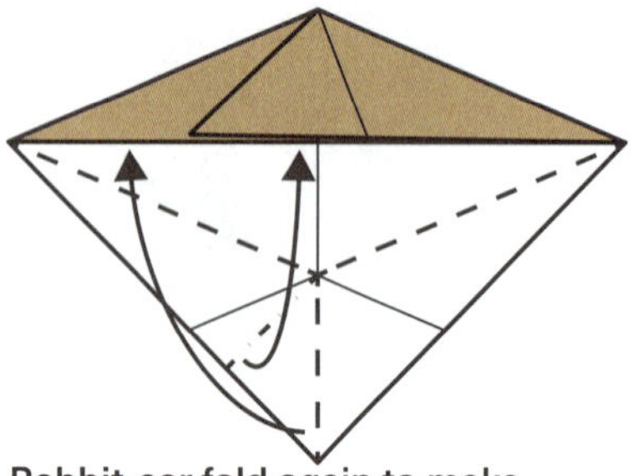

Rabbit-ear fold again to make Fish Base

6

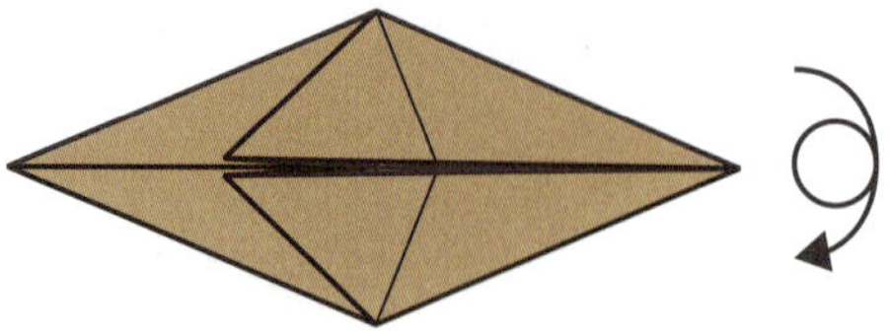

Turn over

7

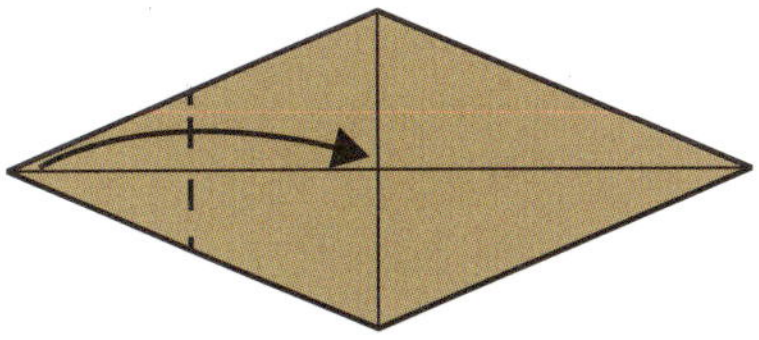

8

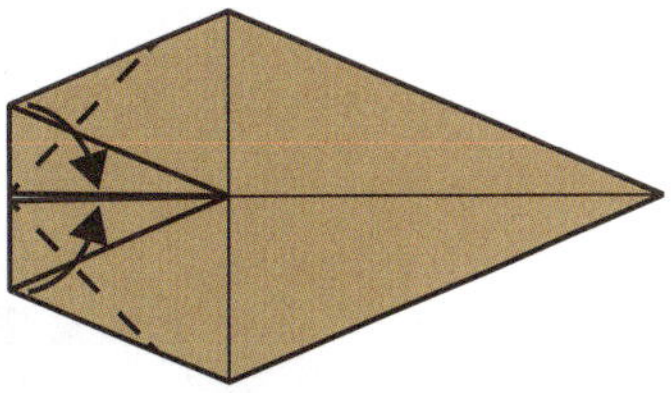

Kite fold

9

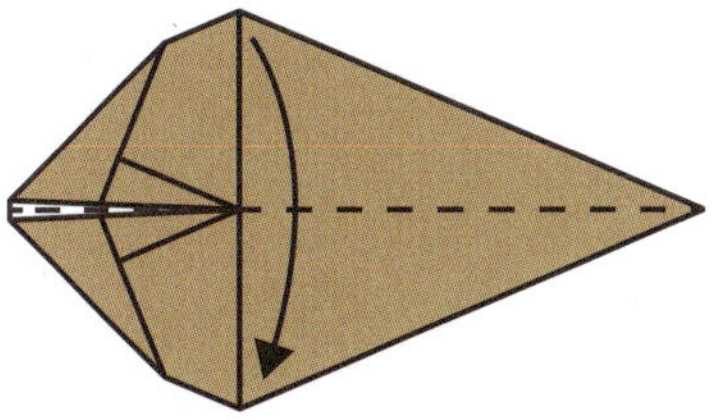

Fold in half

10

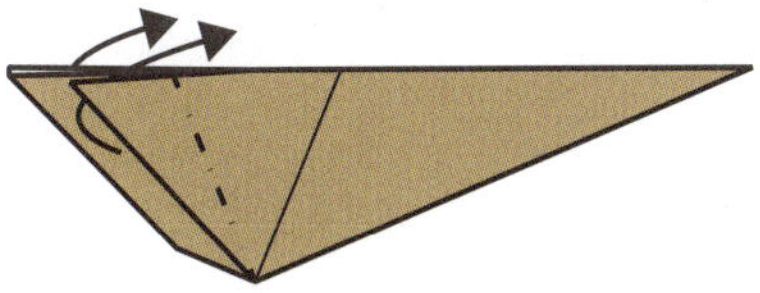

Fold behind
Repeat behind

11

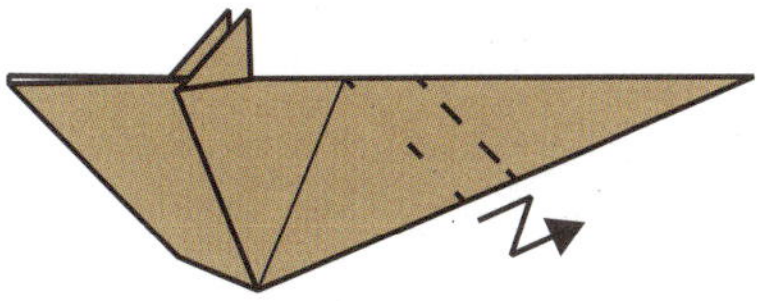

Pleat fold

12

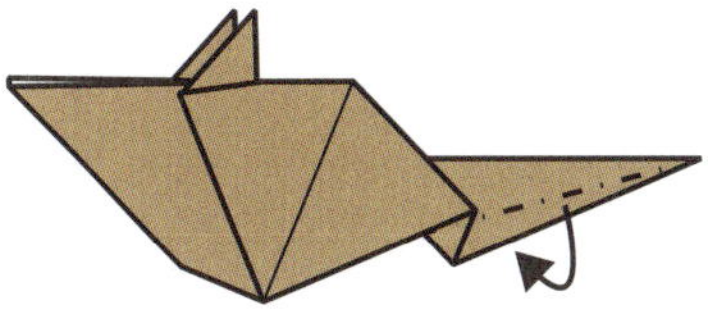

13

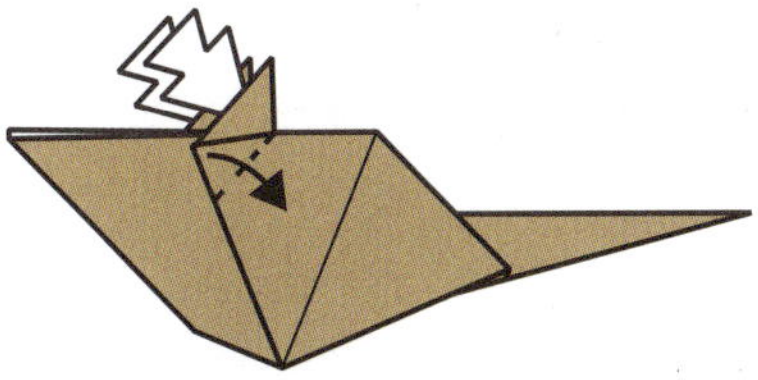

Open to shape
Repeat behind

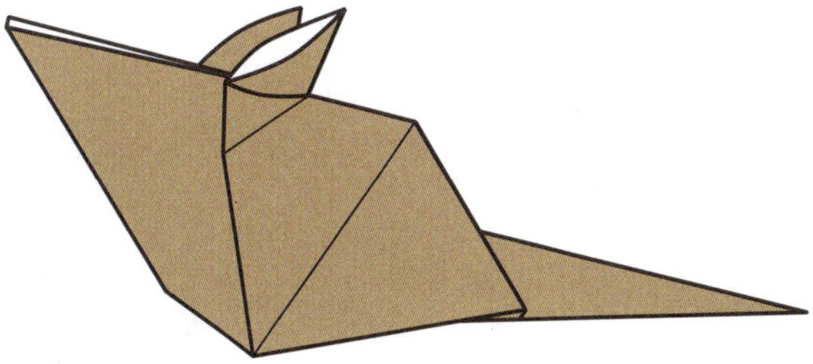

Mouse

Sleeping Bat

- Diagonal Fold
- Kite Fold
- Pleat Fold

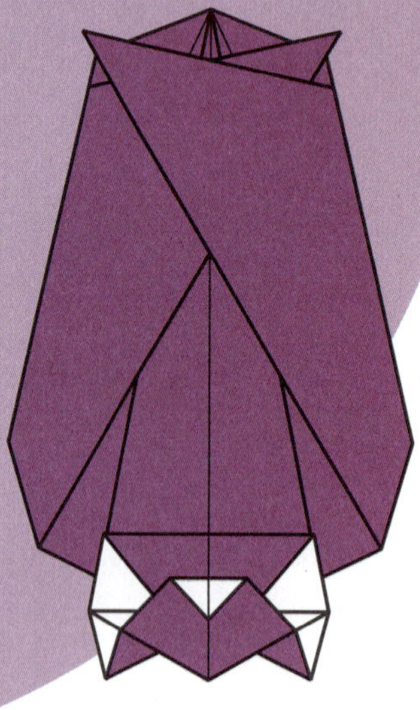

1

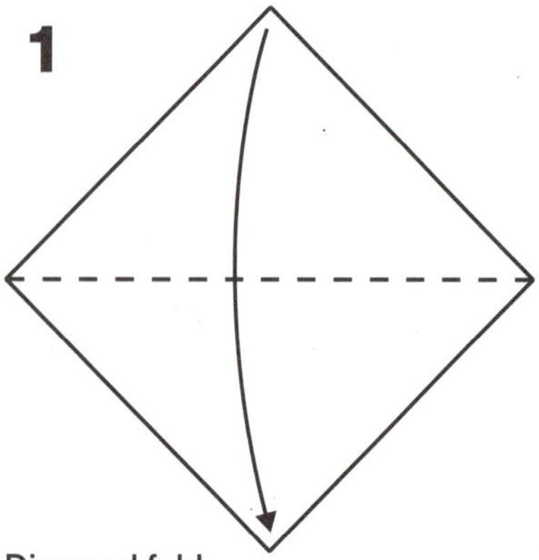

Diagonal fold

2

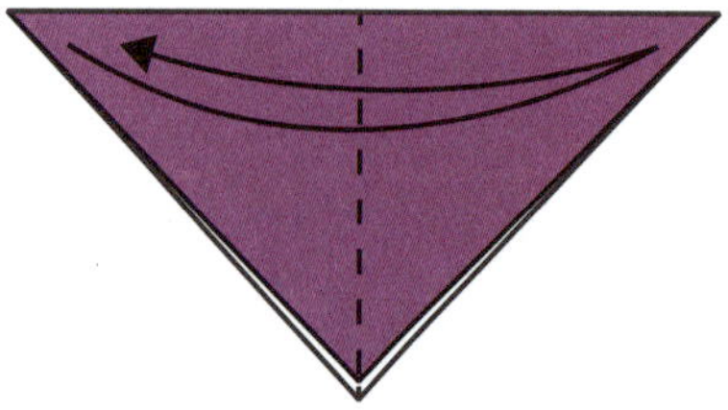

Fold and unfold

3

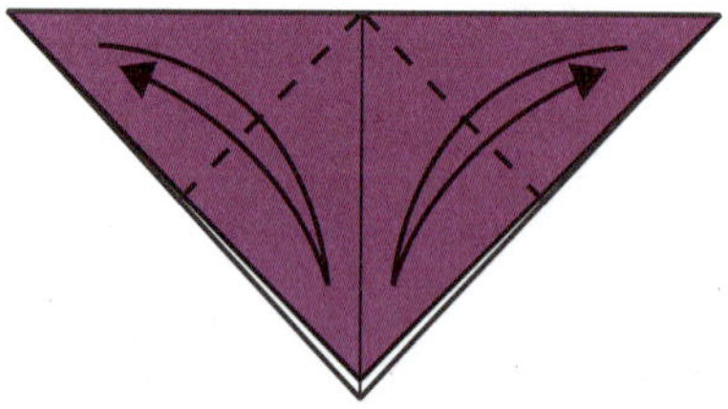

Kite fold and unfold to make pre-creases

4

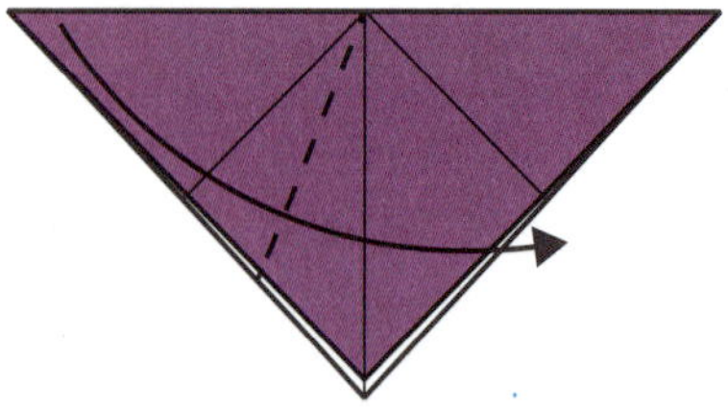

Fold pre-crease to centerline

5

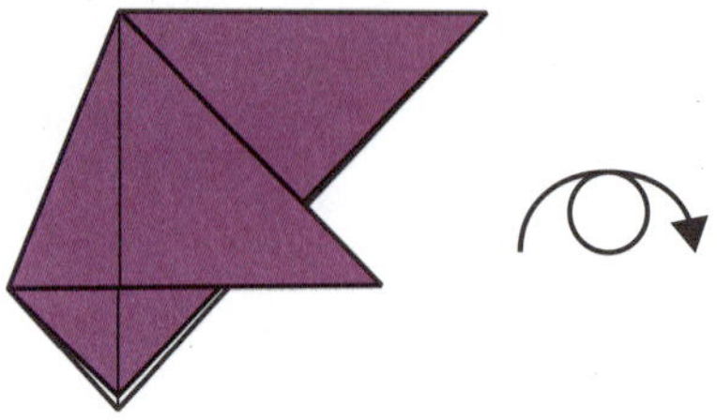

Turn over

6

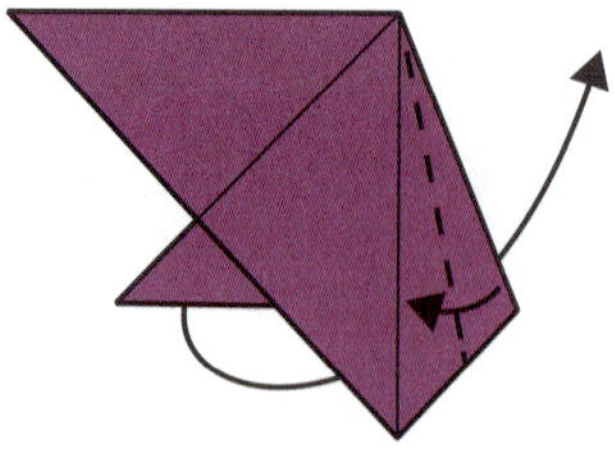

Kite fold and bring flap behind out

7

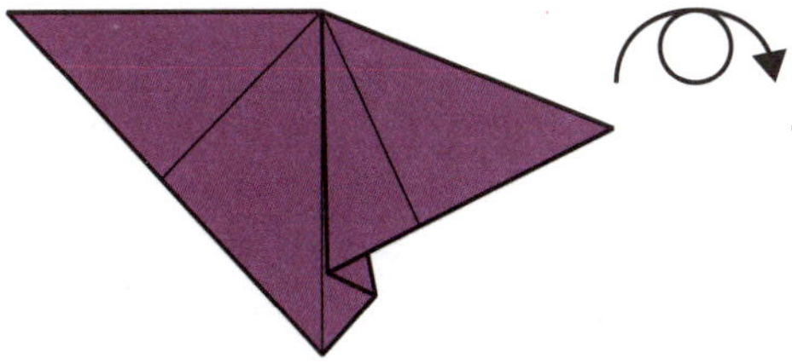

Turn over

8

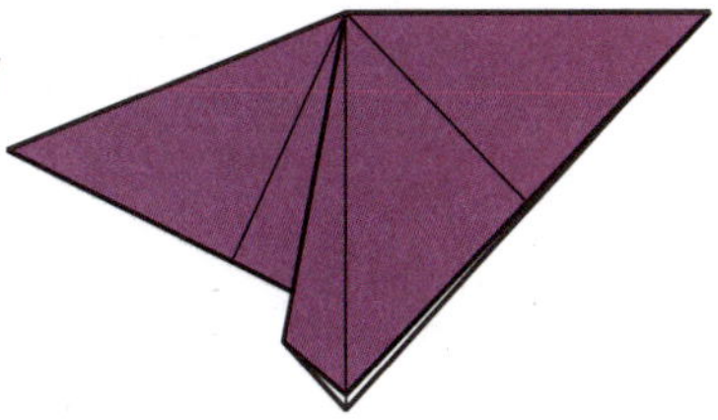

Repeat steps 4-7 on the other side

9

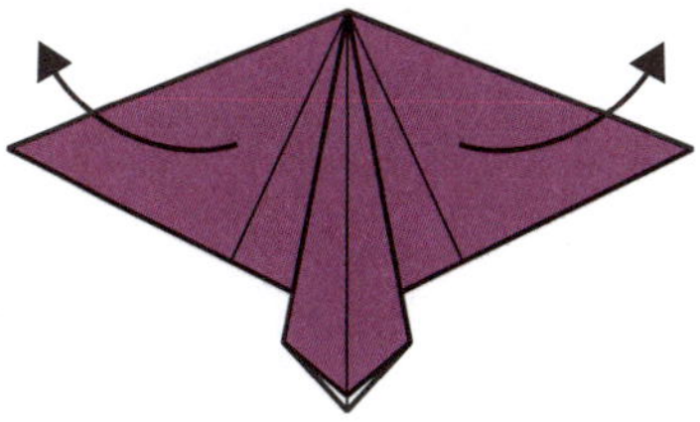

Unfold pleat folds

10

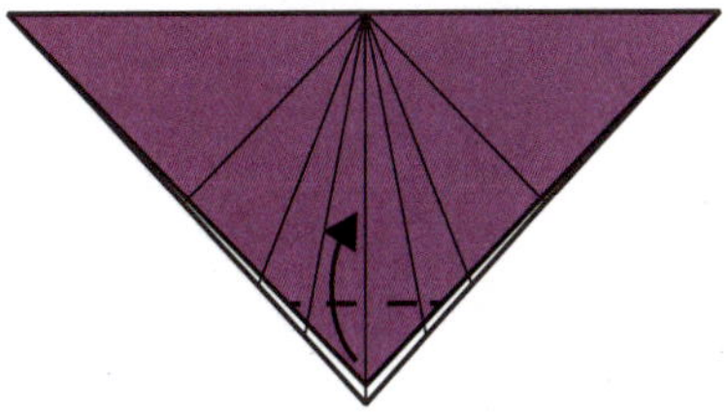

Fold top flap up

11

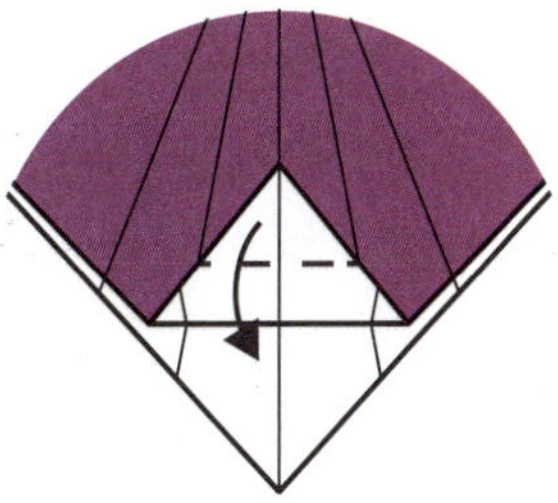

Enlarged view shown
Fold using creases as reference

12

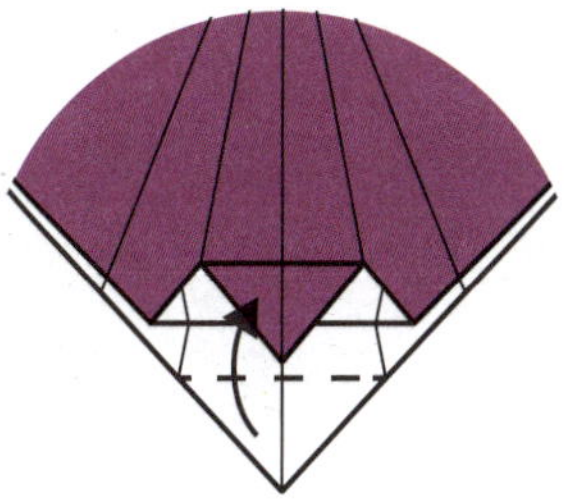

Fold using creases as reference

13

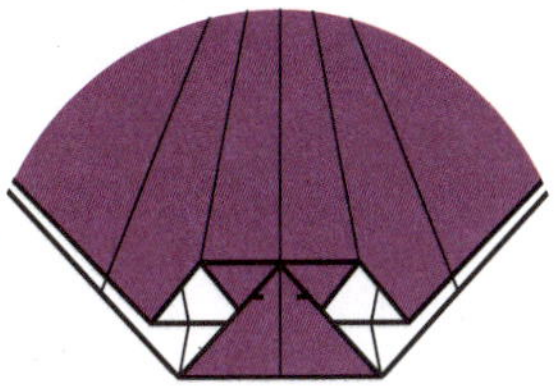

Fold tip down

14

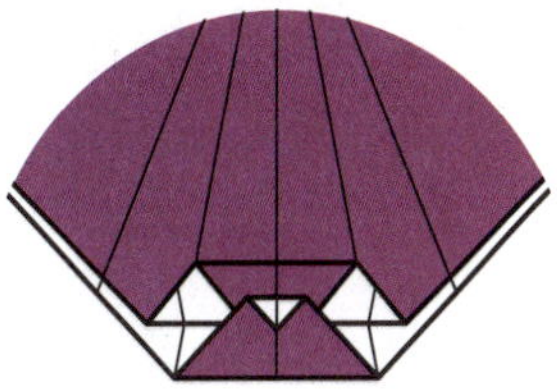

15

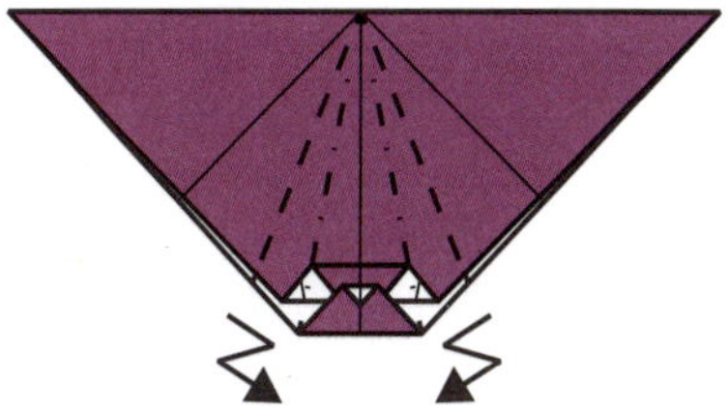

Refold pleat folds

16

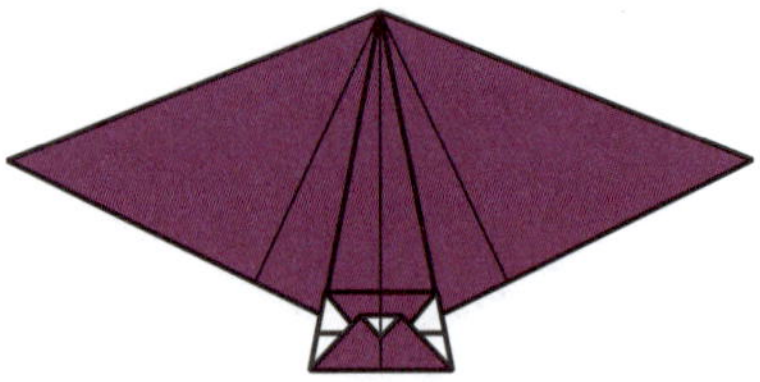

17

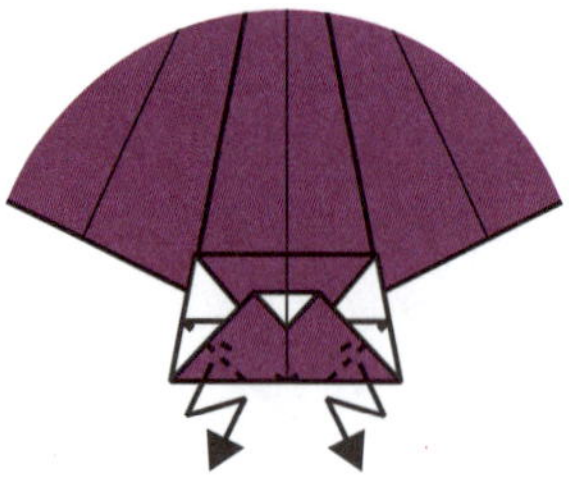

Enlarged view shown
Pleat fold corners

18

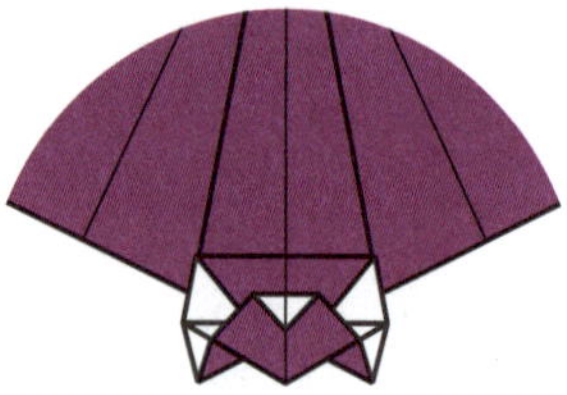

19

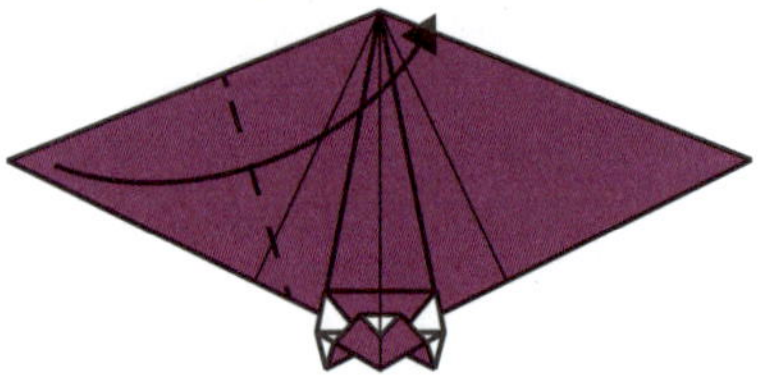

20

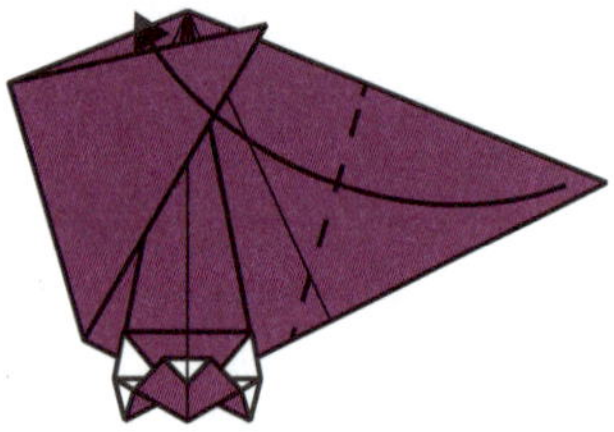

21

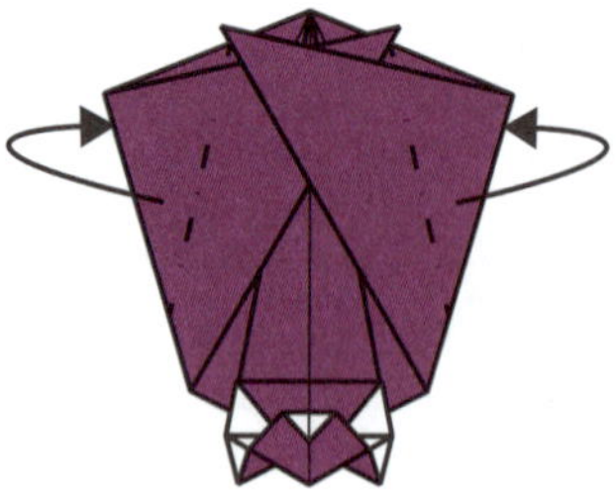

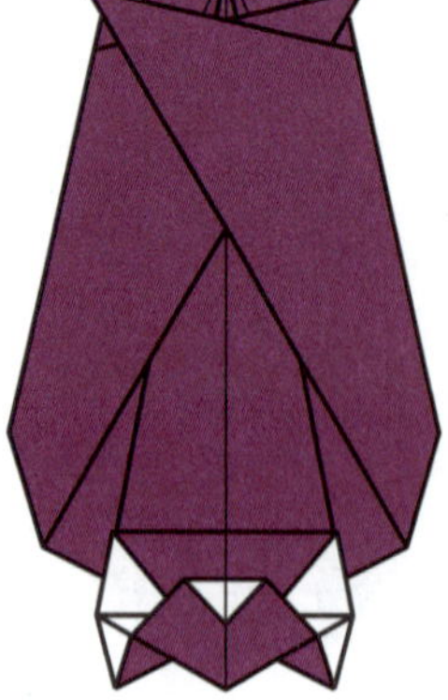

Sleeping Bat

Chrysanthemum

- Book Fold
- Diagonal Fold
- Kite Fold
- Cabinet Fold
- Squash Fold

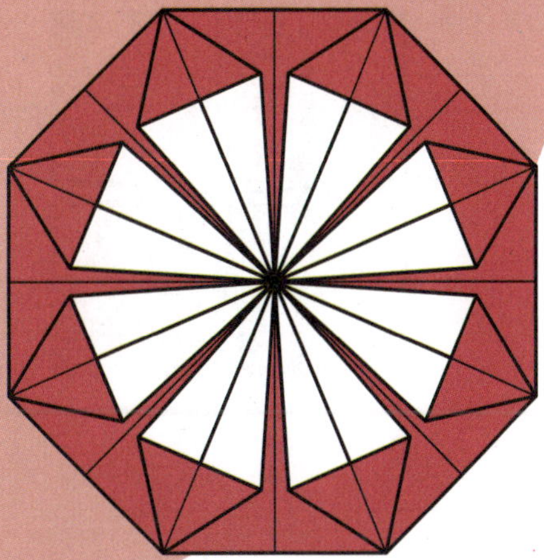

1

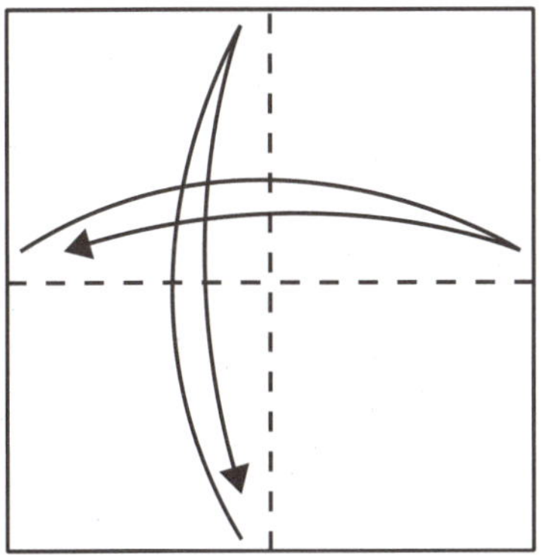

Book fold and unfold twice

2

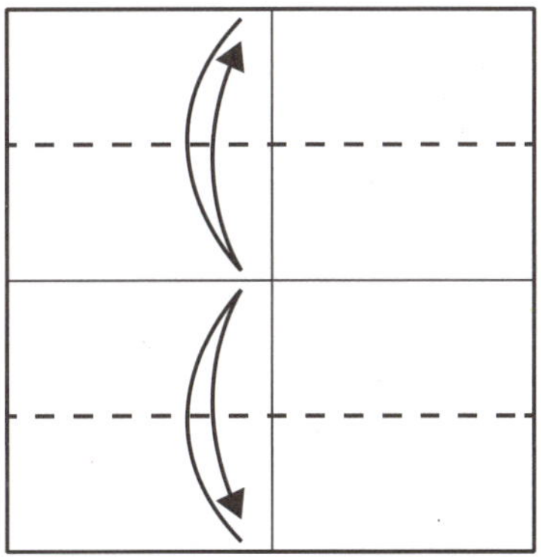

Cabinet fold and unfold

3

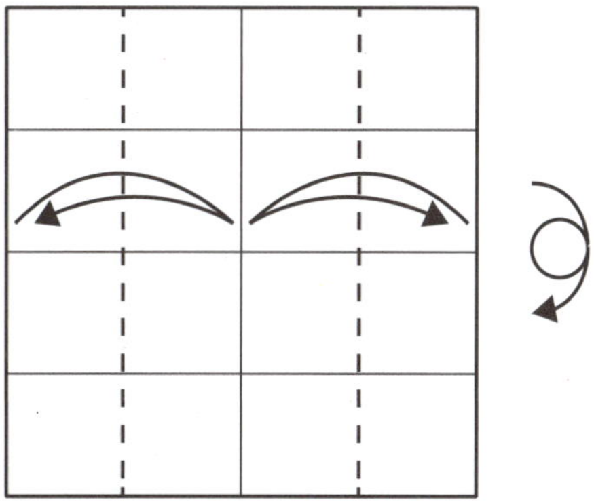

Cabinet fold and unfold again
Turn over

4

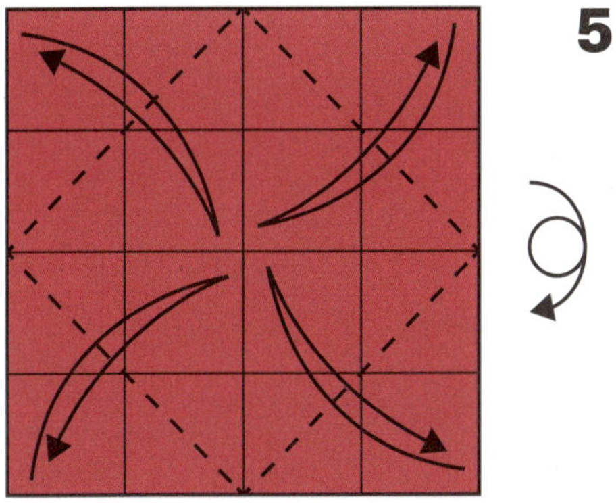

Blintz fold and unfold
Turn over

5

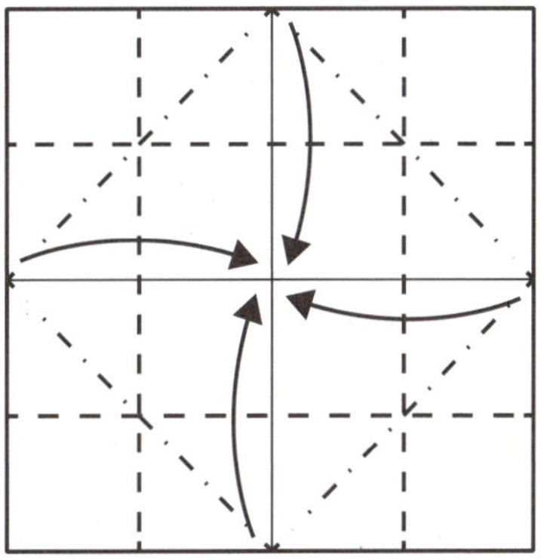

Begin to collapse

6

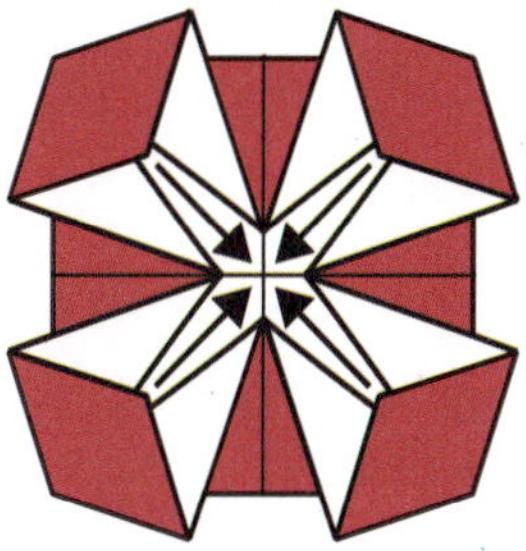

3D step in progress
Continue to collapse

7

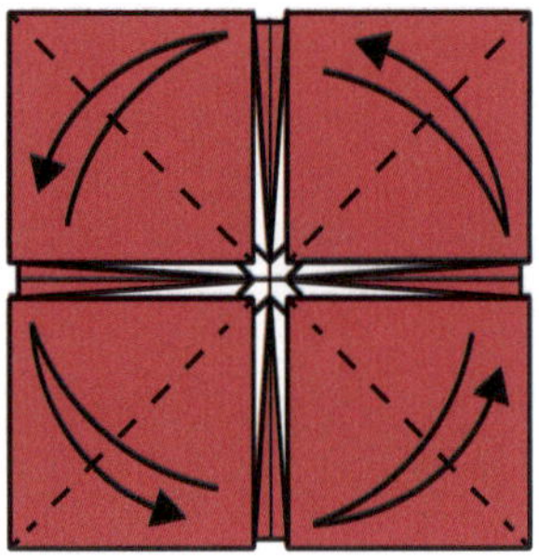

Diagonal fold and unfold four times

8

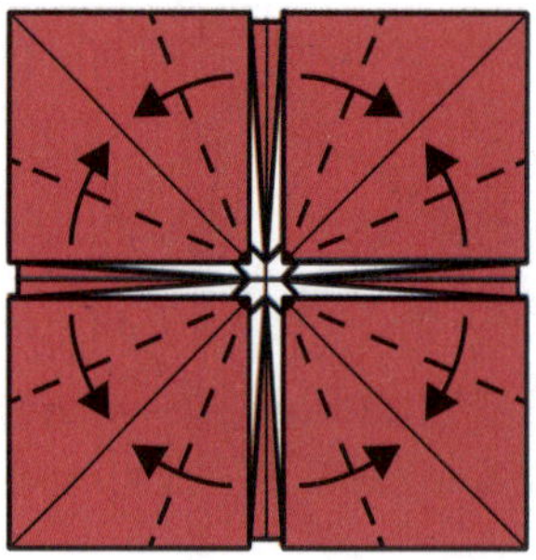

Kite fold all flaps

9

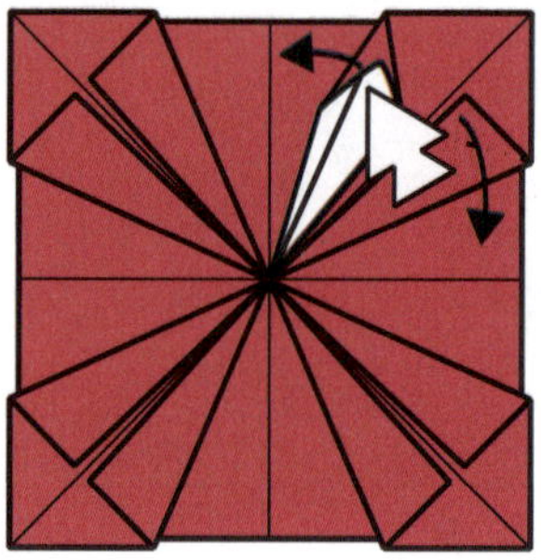

Squash fold both flaps

10

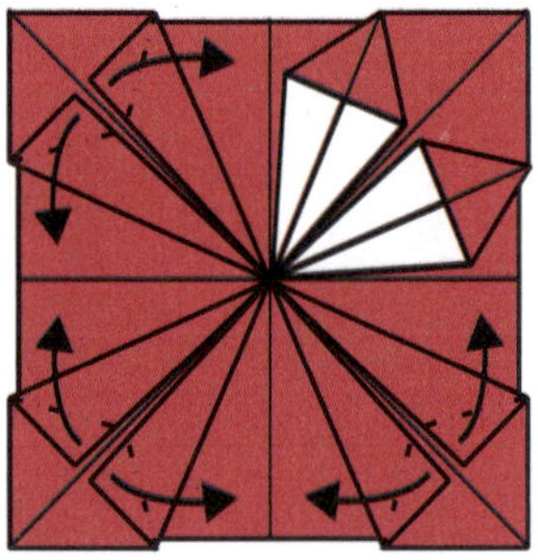

Repeat on remaining flaps

11

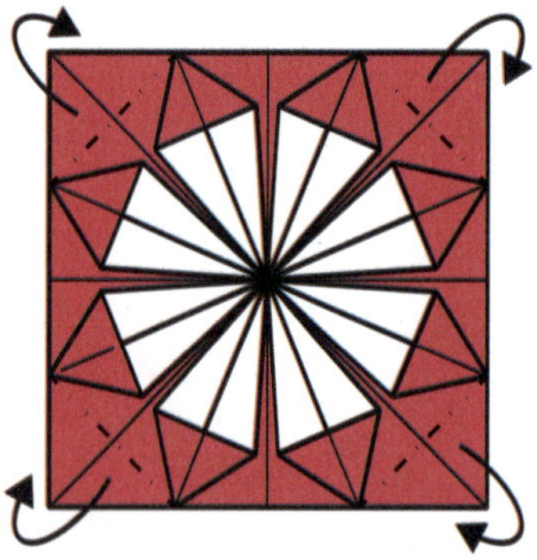

Fold four corners behind

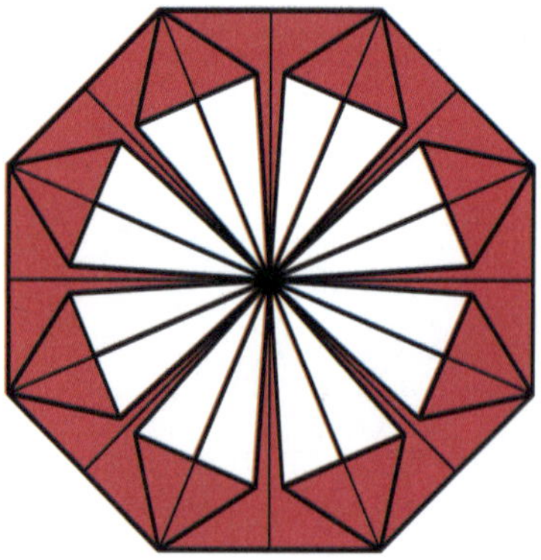

Chrysanthemum

Bowl

- Diagonal Fold
- Kite Fold
- Pleat Fold

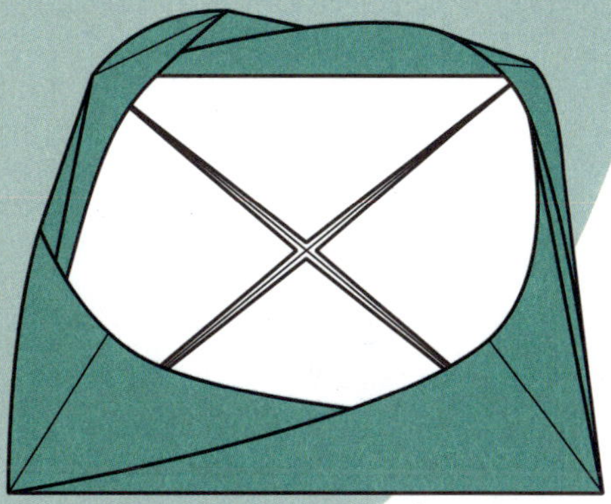

1

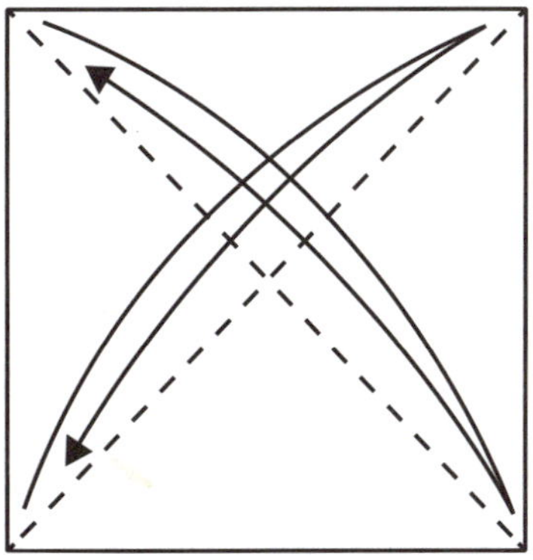

Diagonal fold and unfold twice

2

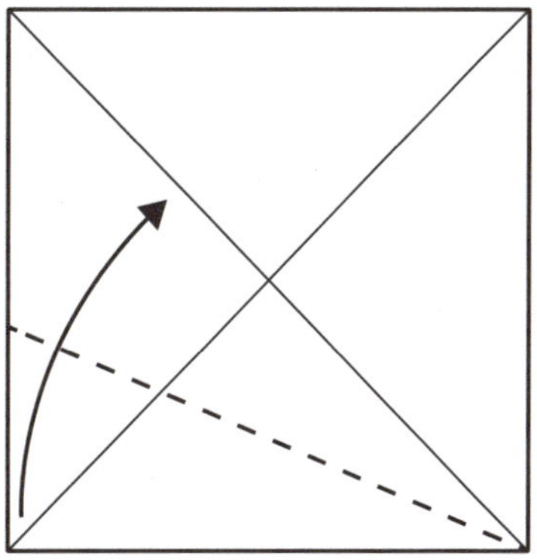

Kite fold

3

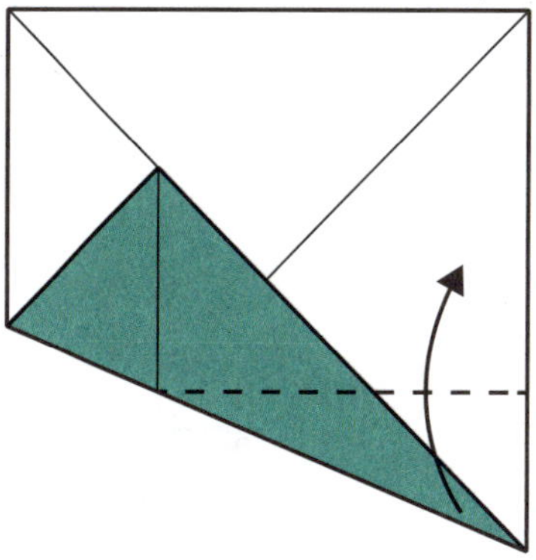

4

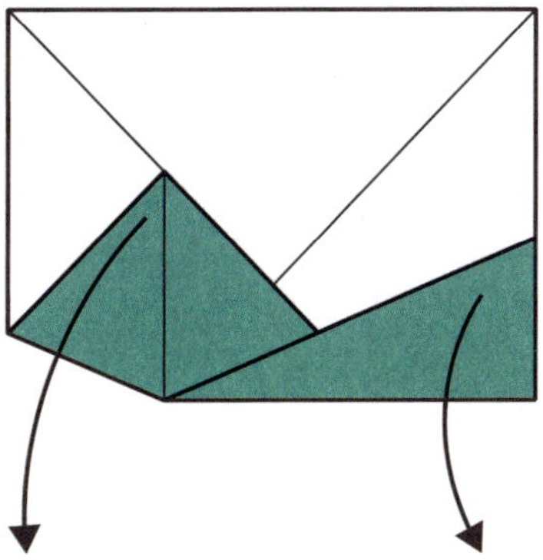

Unfold

5

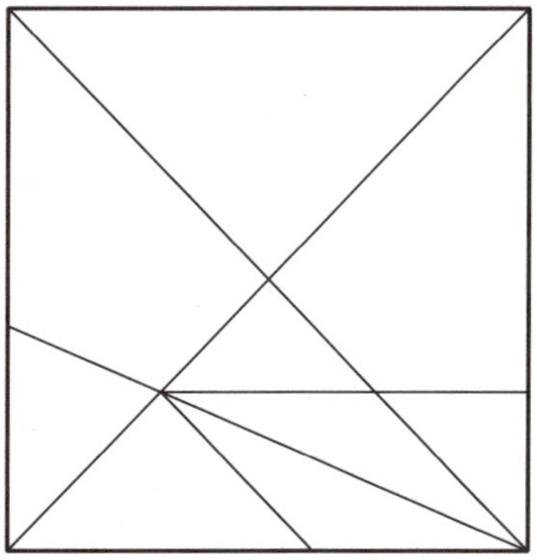

Rotate

6

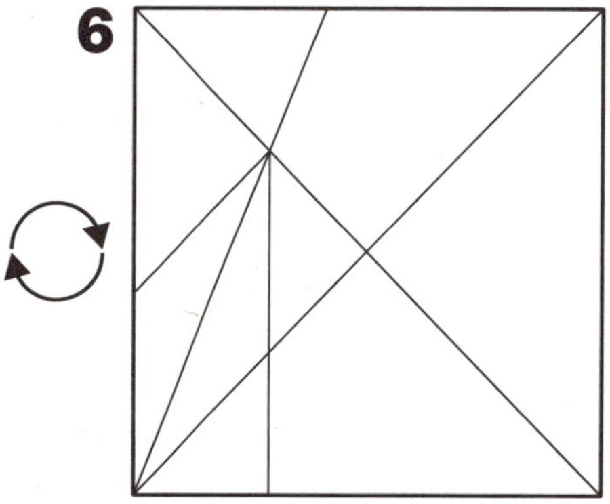

Repeat steps 2-5 three sides

7

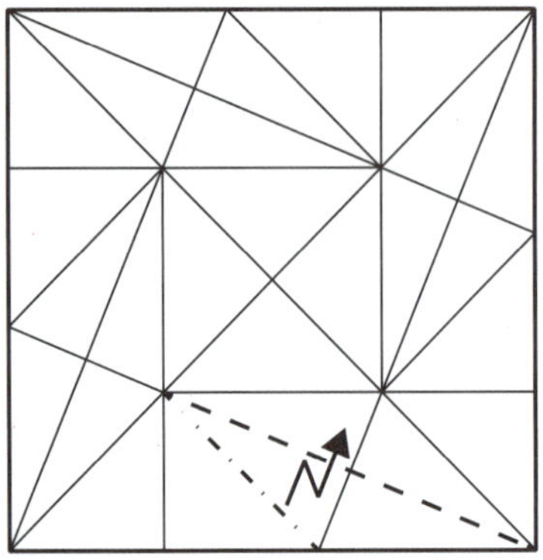

Pleat fold
Section becomes 3D

8

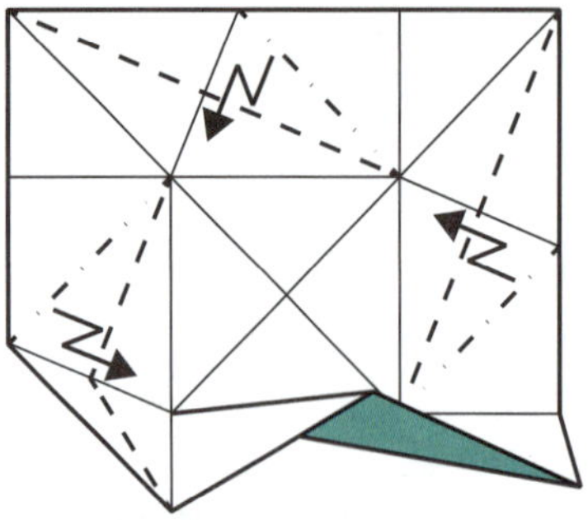

Pleat fold three more times
counterclockwise
All sections will be 3D

9

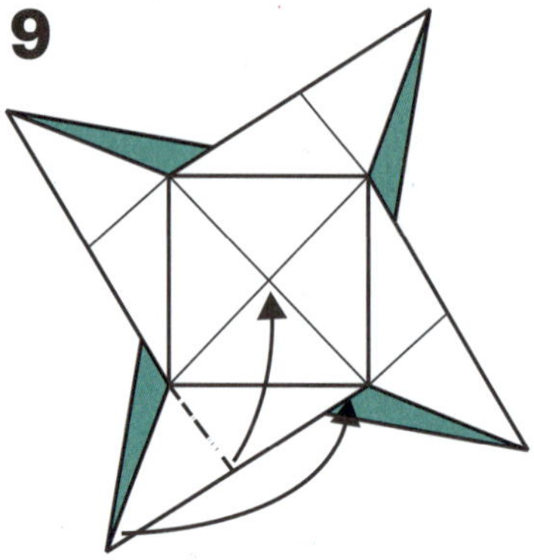

10

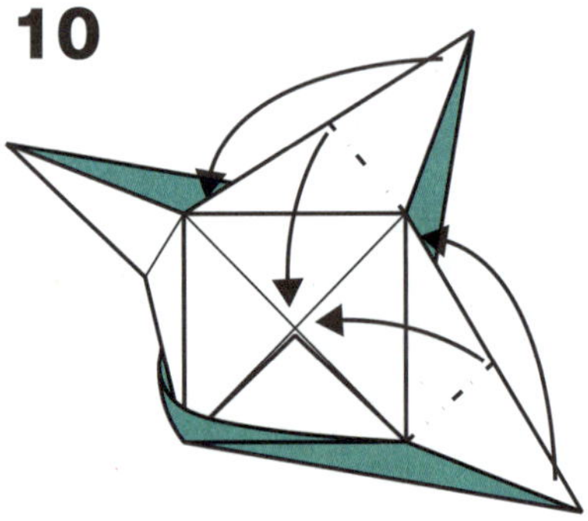

Continue counterclockwise

11

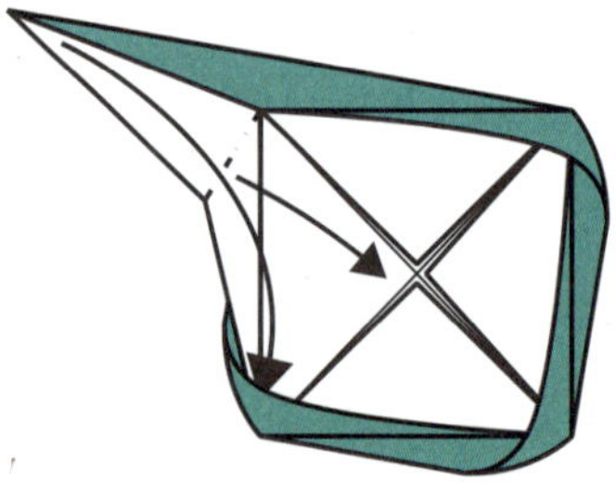

Tuck in final section

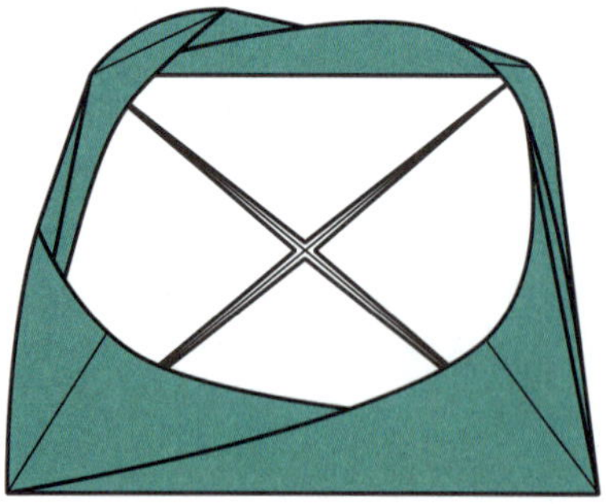

Bowl

Butterfly

- Book Fold
- Cabinet Fold
- Diagonal Fold
- Kite Fold
- Pleat Fold
- Squash Fold

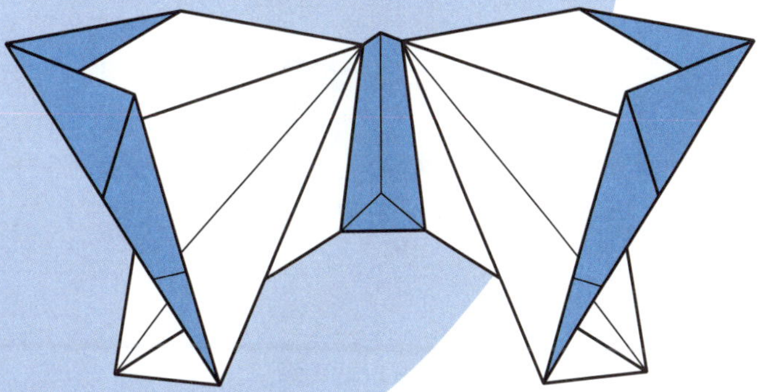

1

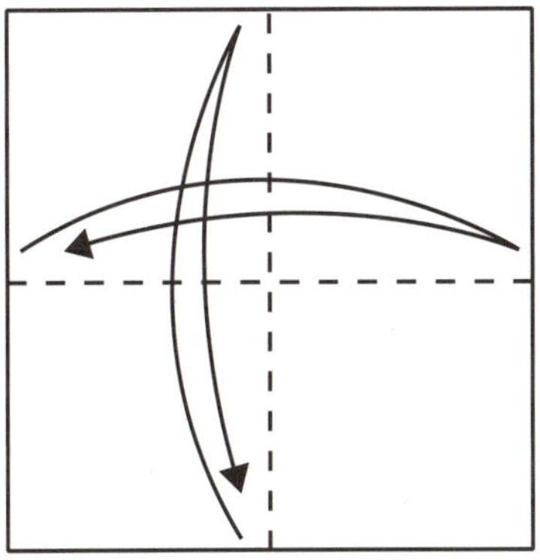

Book fold and unfold twice

2

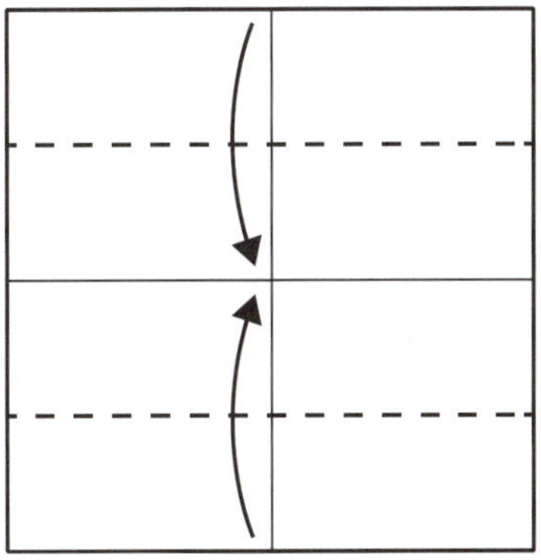

Cabinet fold

3

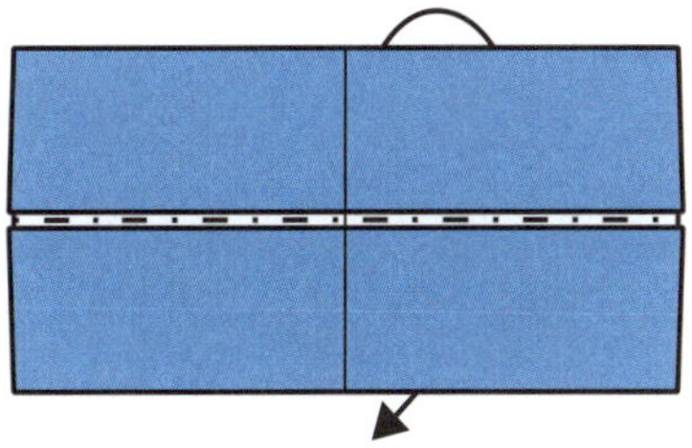

Book fold behind

4

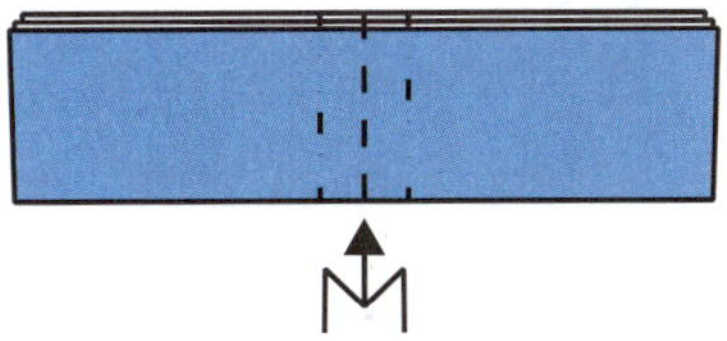

Pleat fold
Center line will be 3D

5

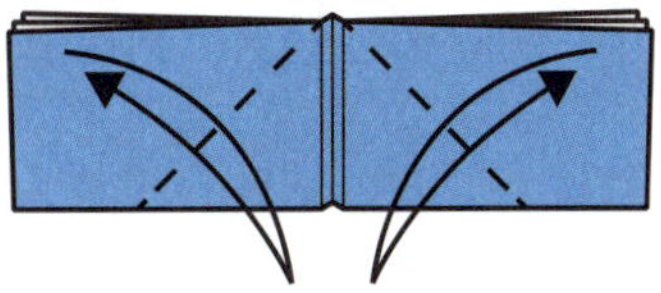

Kite fold and unfold

6

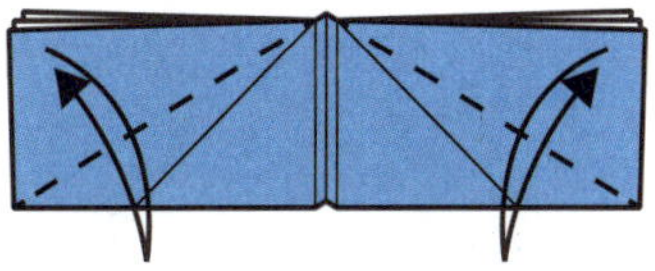

7

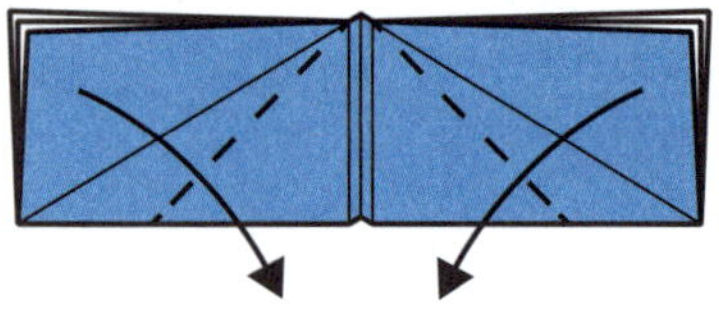

Squash folds

8

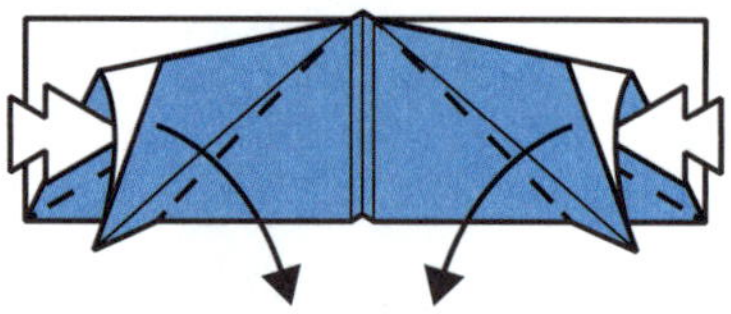

3D step in progress

9

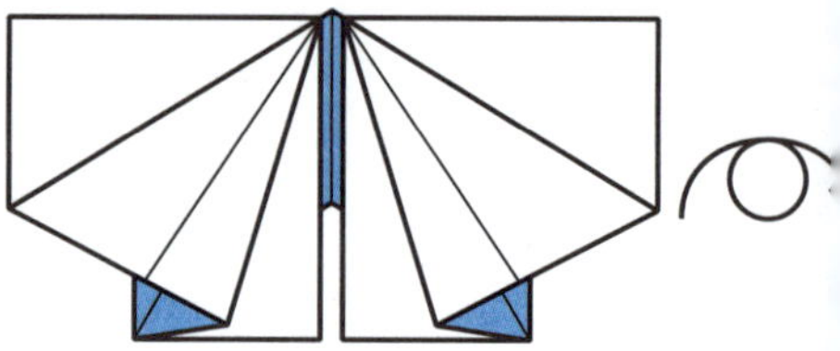

Turn over

10

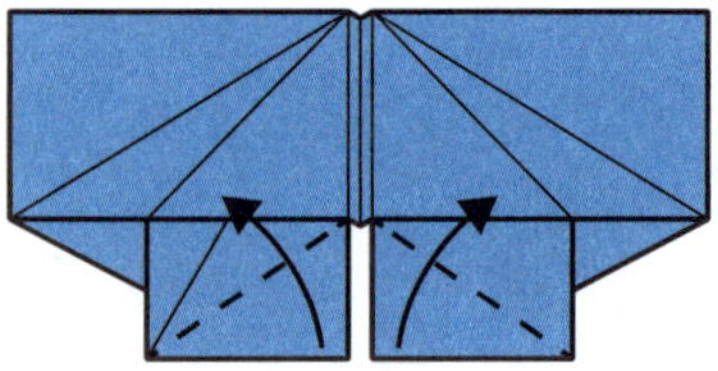

11

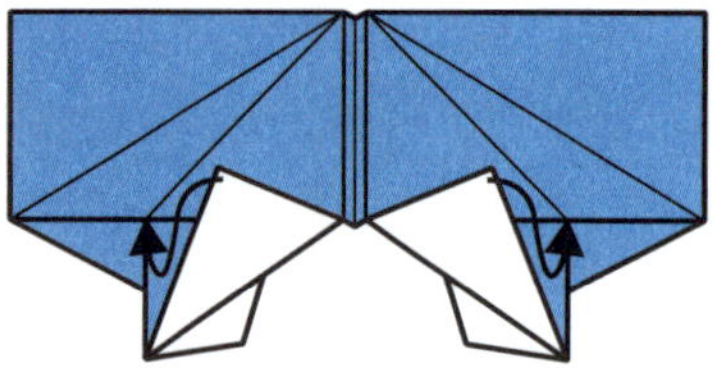

Tuck corners under edges

12

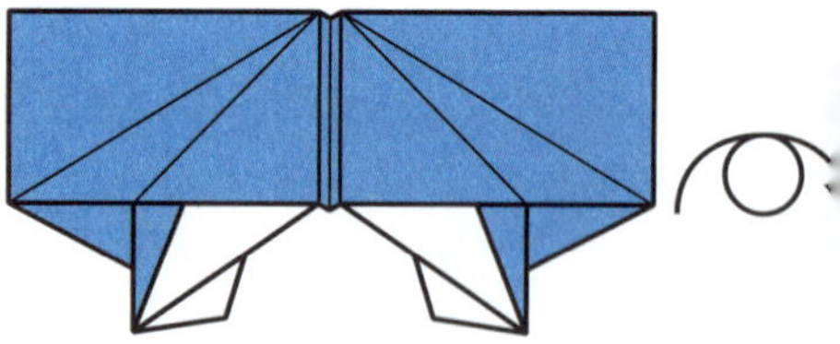

Turn over

13

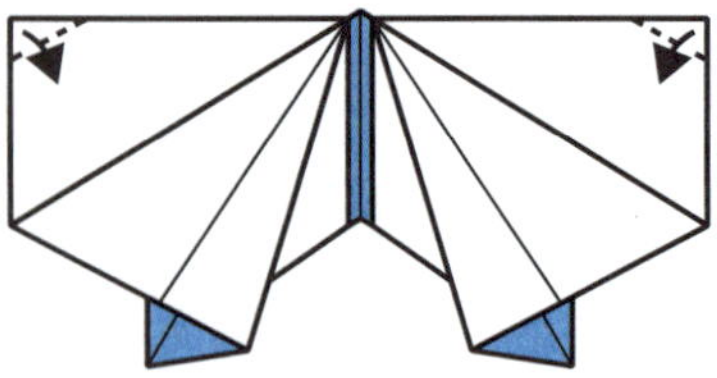

14

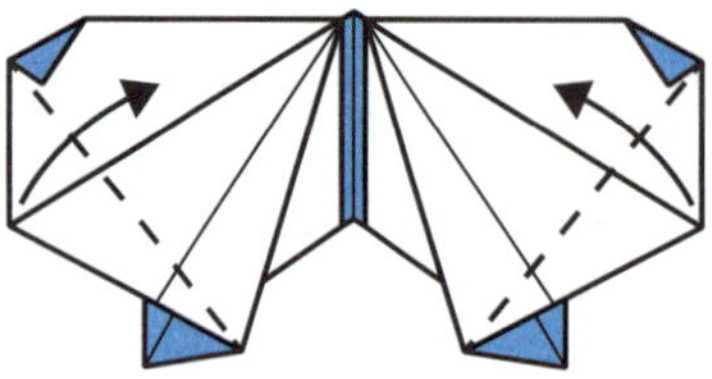

15

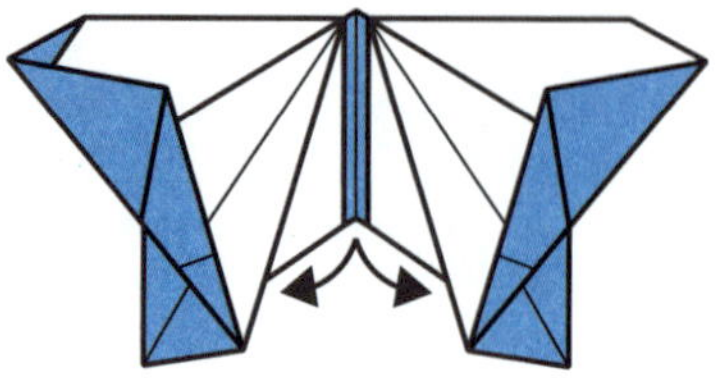

Spread apart pleat at bottom

16

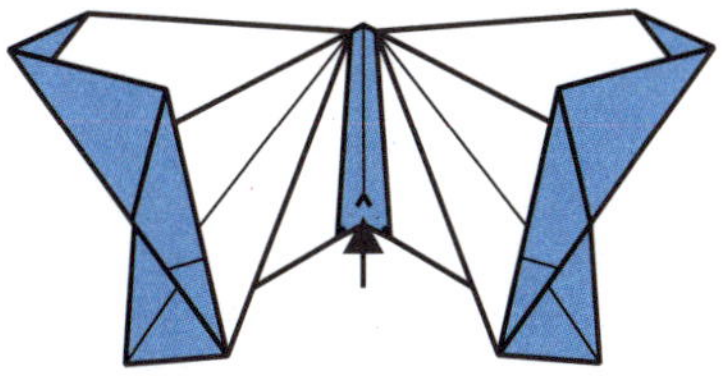

Squash fold

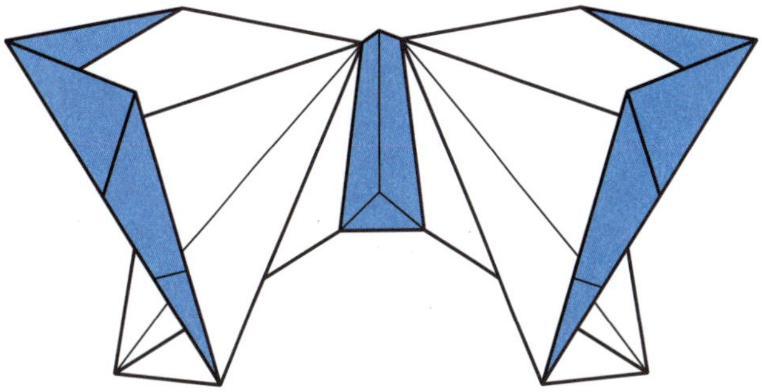

Butterfly

Rabbit

- Book Fold
- Diagonal Fold
- Cabinet Fold
- Kite Fold
- Squash Fold
- Inside Reverse Fold

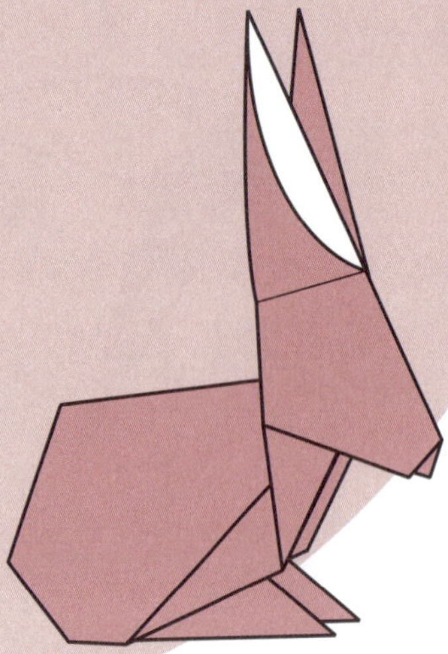

1

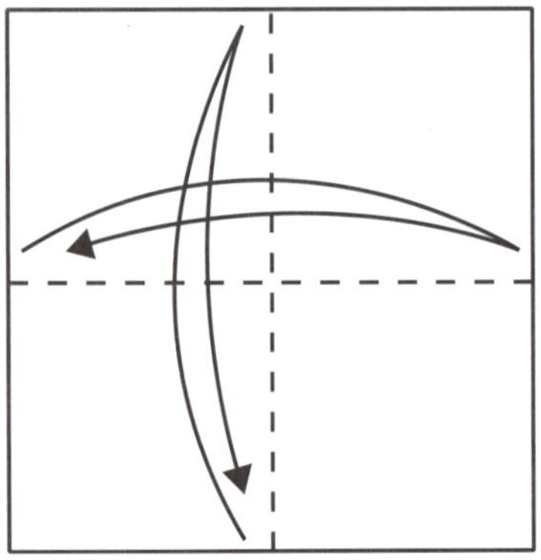

Book fold and unfold twice

2

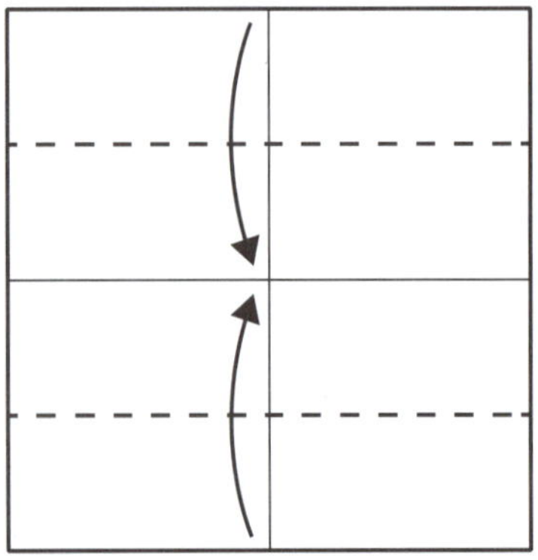

Cabinet fold

3

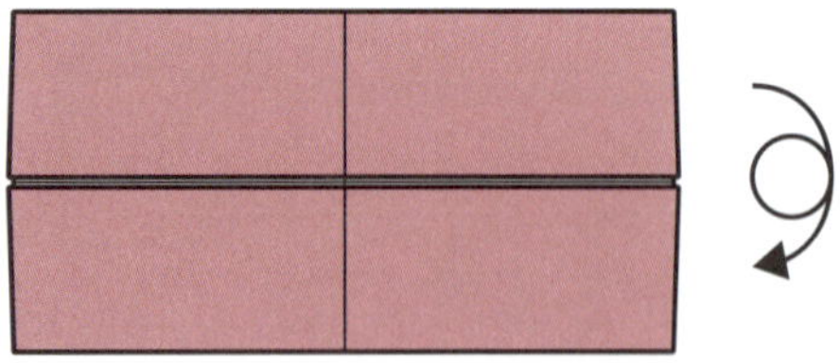

Turn over

4

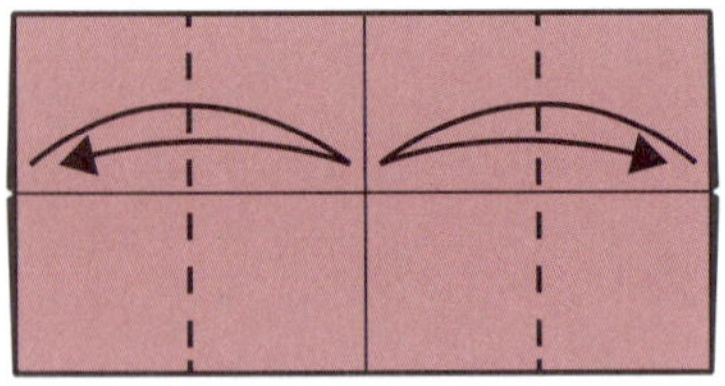

Cabinet fold and unfold

5

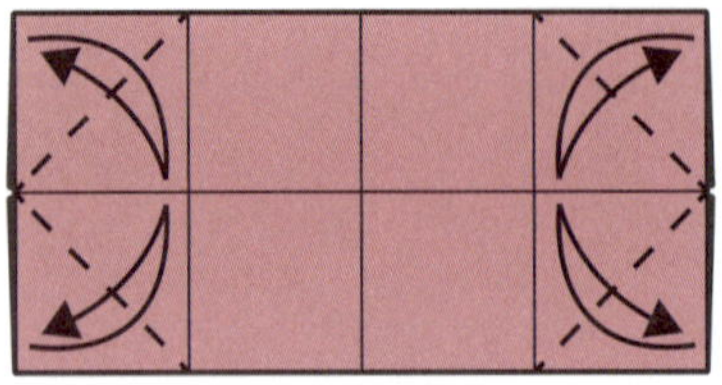

Kite fold and unfold

6

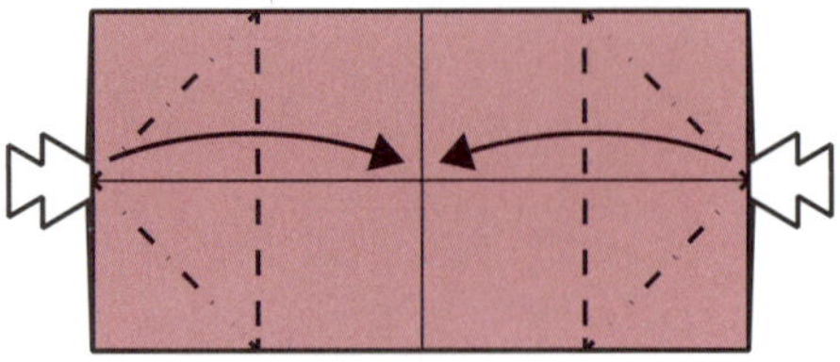

Open from sides and squash fold

7

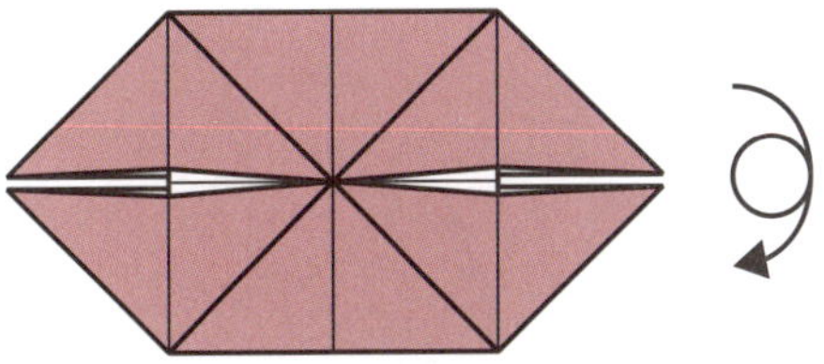

Turn over

8

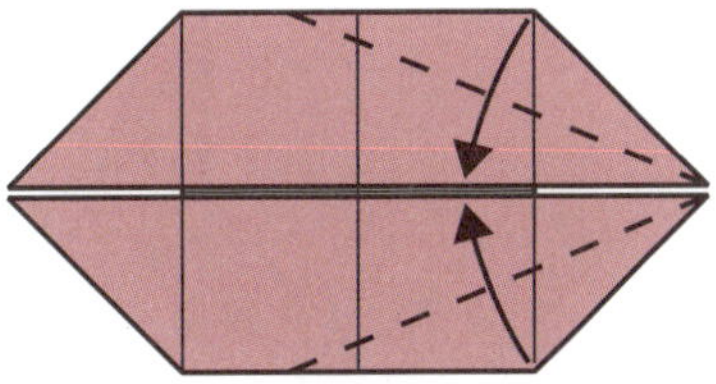

Kite fold

9

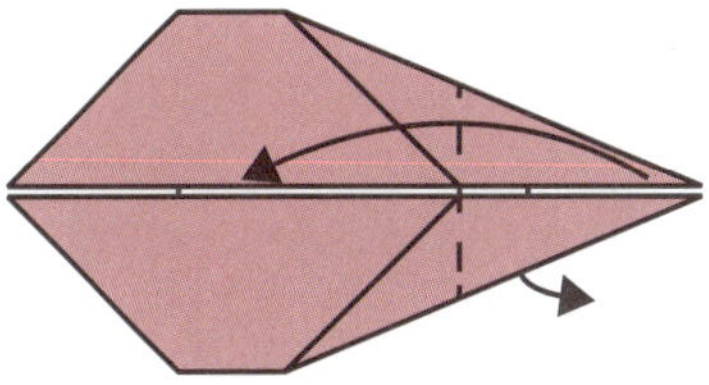

Fold over and bring hidden flap out

10

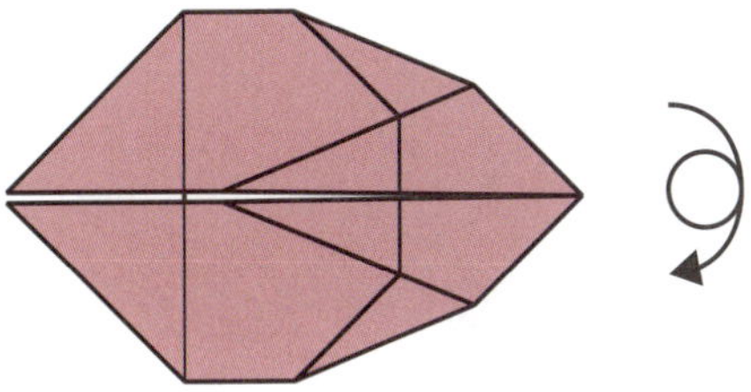

Turn over

11

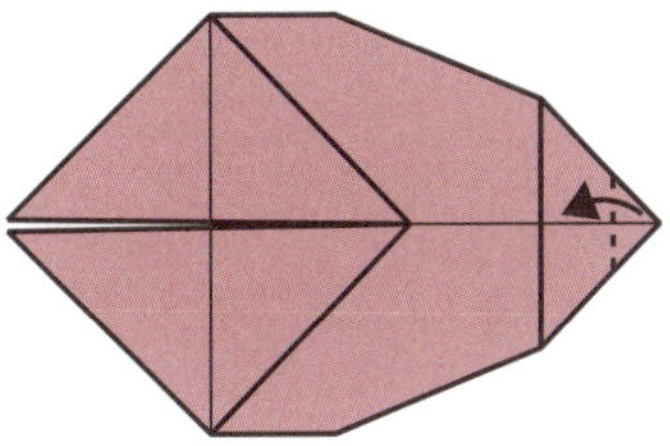

12

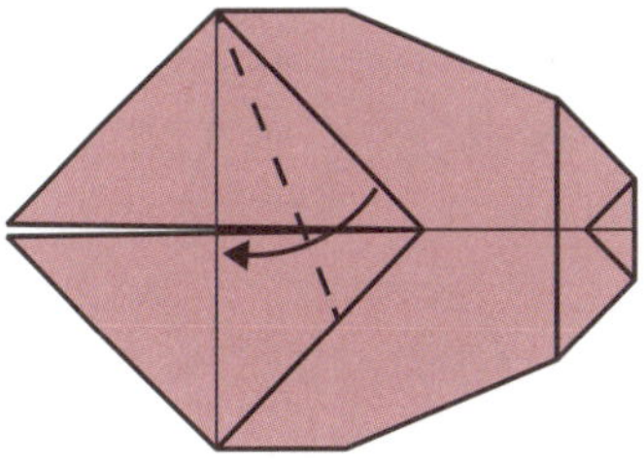

13

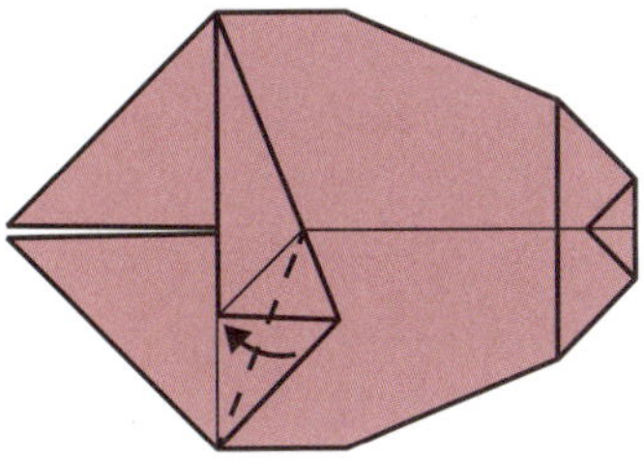

14

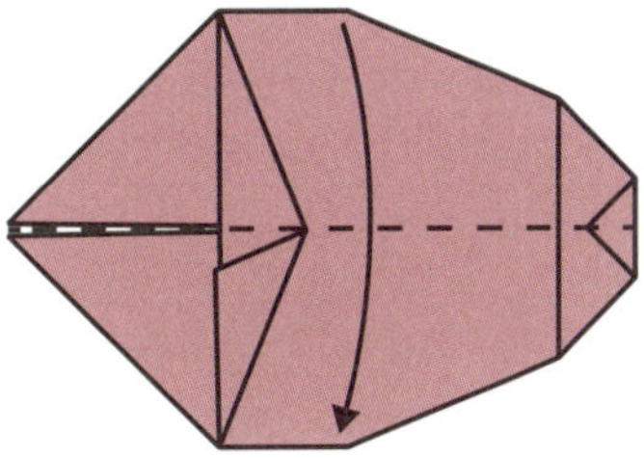

Fold in half

15

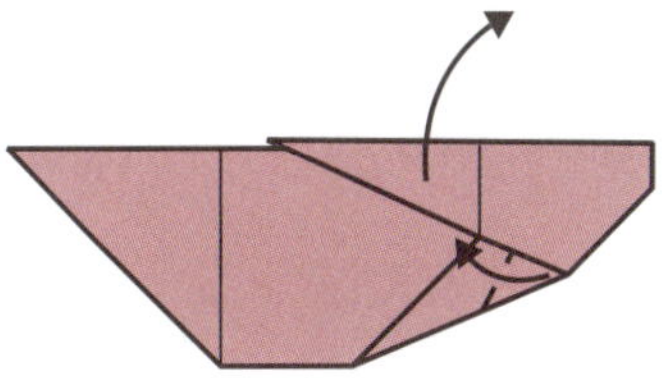

Slide up section

16

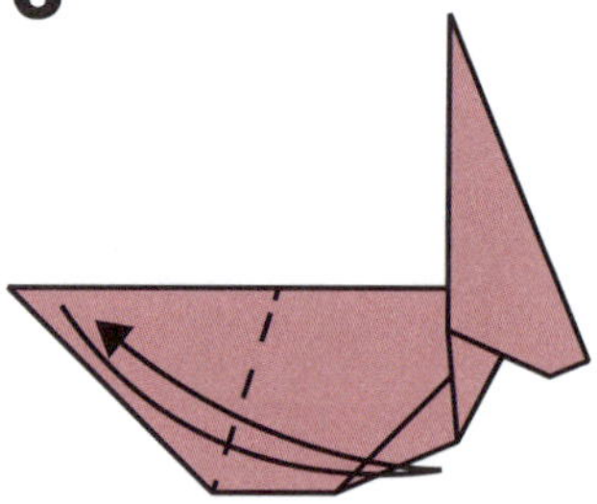

Fold and unfold along hidden edges from steps 12 and 13

17

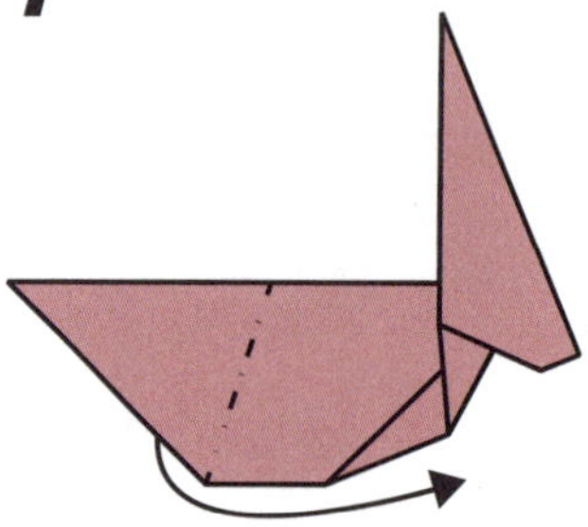

Inside reverse fold

18

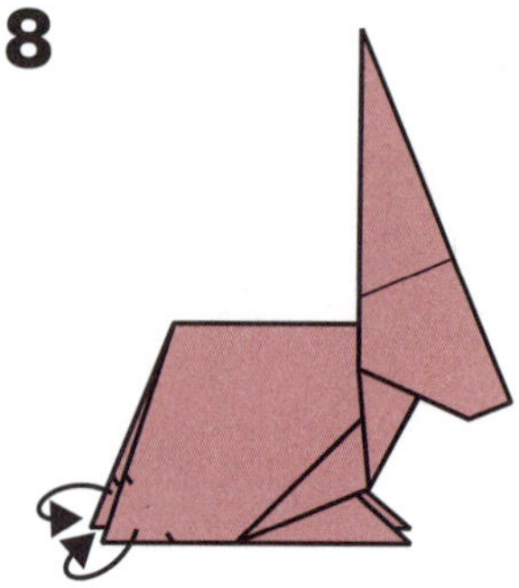

19

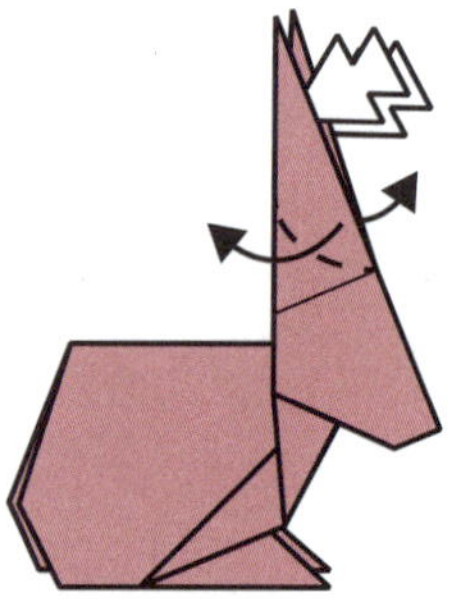

Partially open to shape
Repeat behind

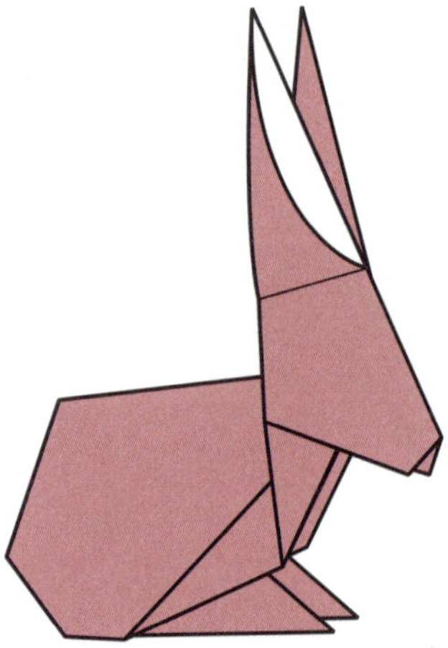

Rabbit

Dragon

- Diagonal Fold
- Kite Fold
- Pleat Fold
- Squash Fold
- Rabbit-ear Fold
- Inside Reverse Fold

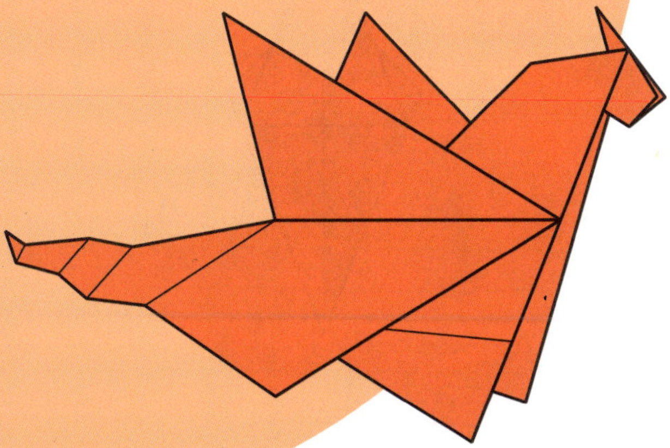

1

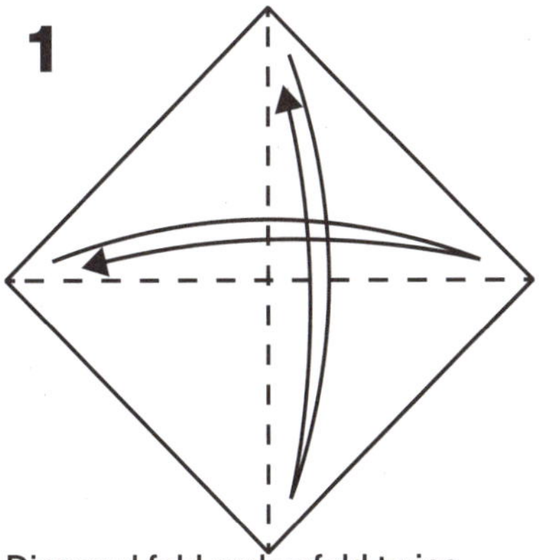

Diagonal fold and unfold twice

2

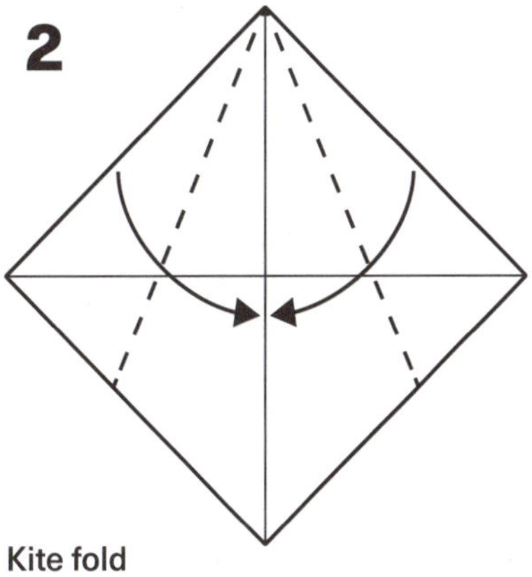

Kite fold

3

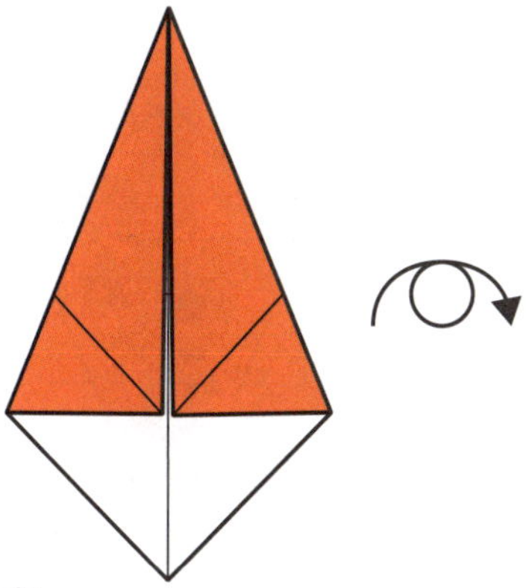

Turn over

4

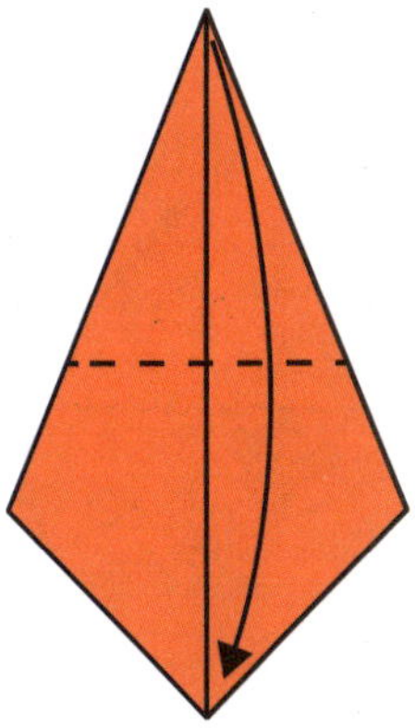

5

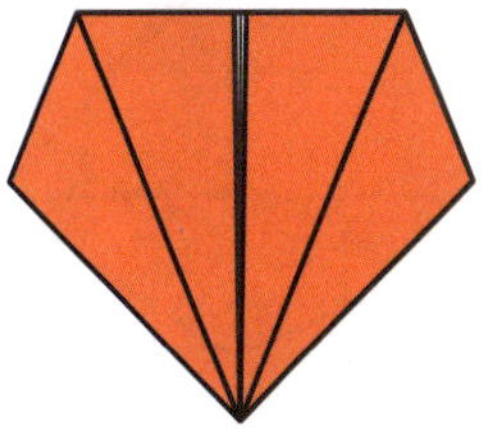

Turn over

6

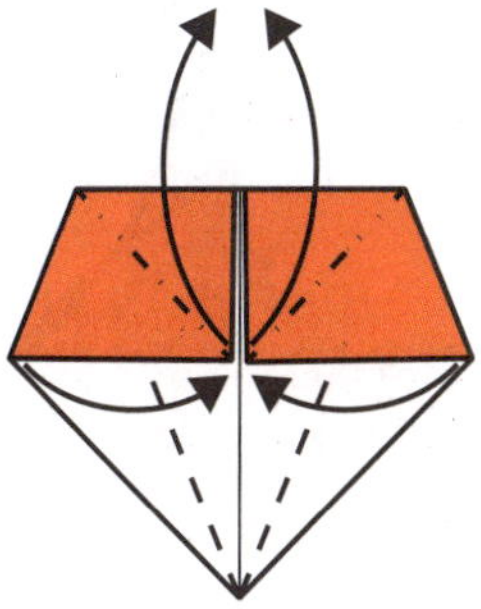

Squash folds

7

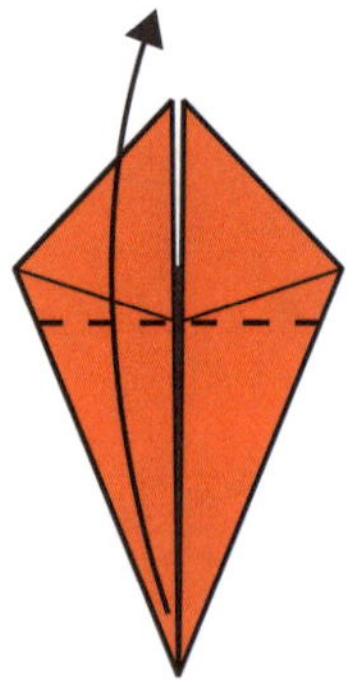

8

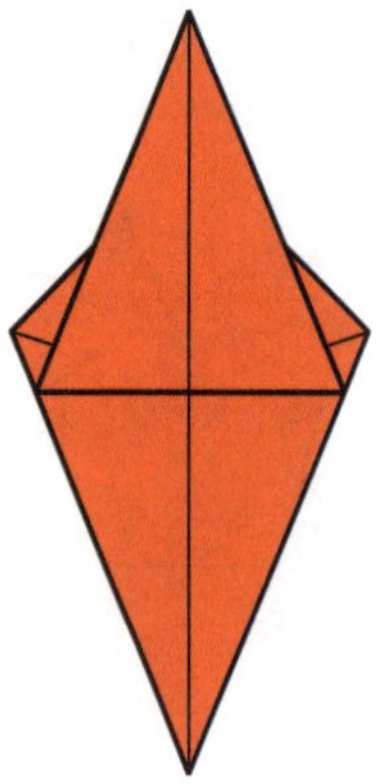

Turn over

9

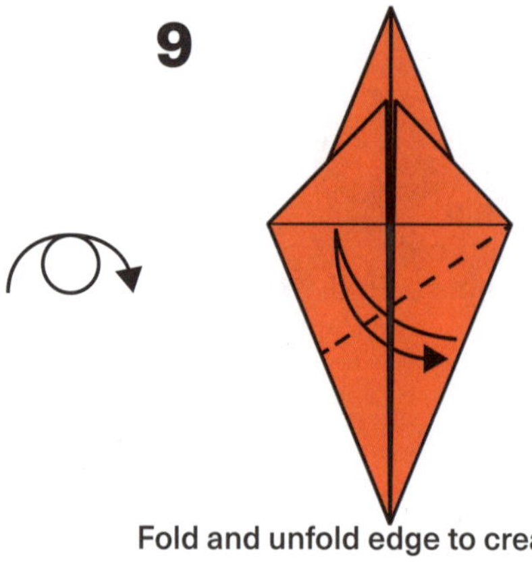

Fold and unfold edge to crease

10

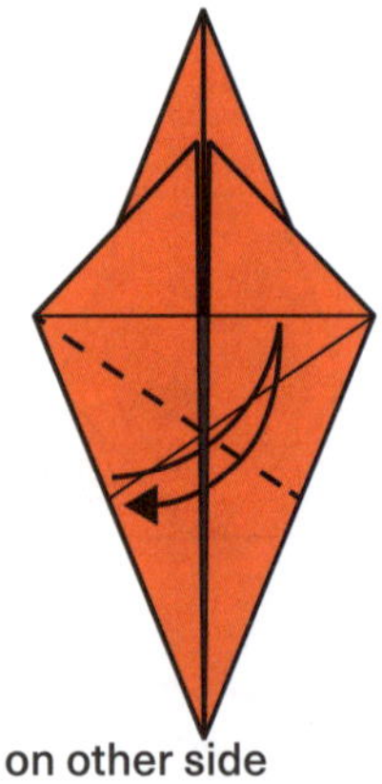

Repeat on other side

11

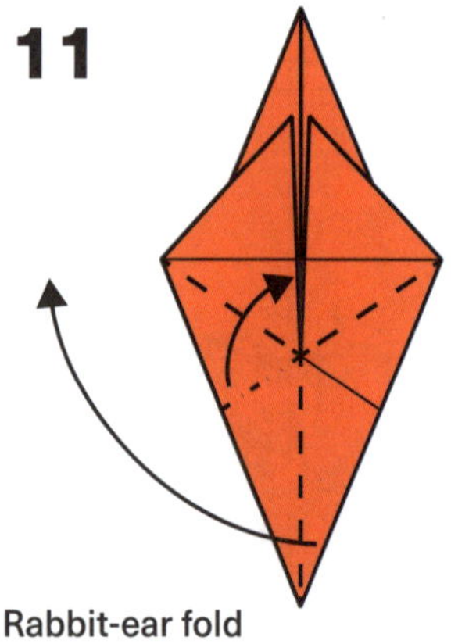

Rabbit-ear fold

12

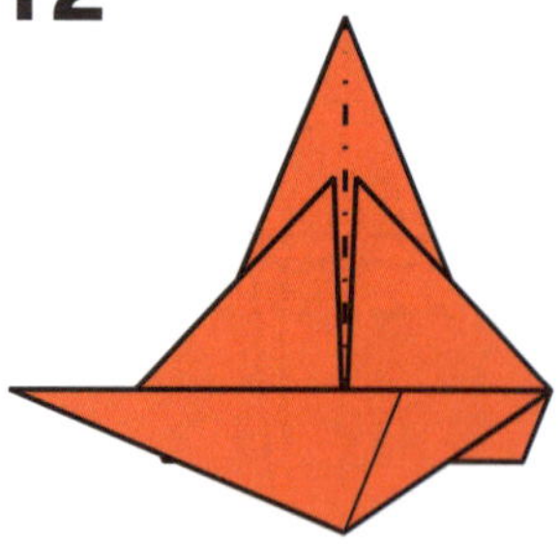

Fold behind

13

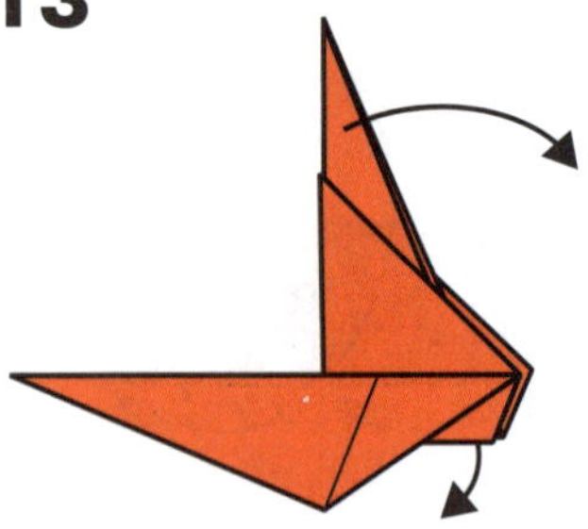

Slide inner section out to line up with edge

14

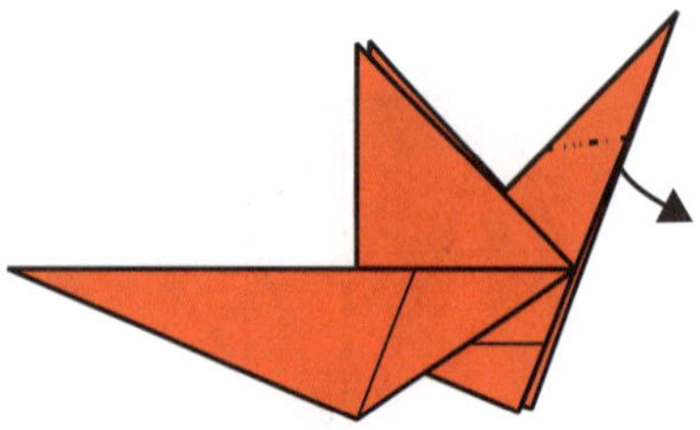

Inside reverse fold

15

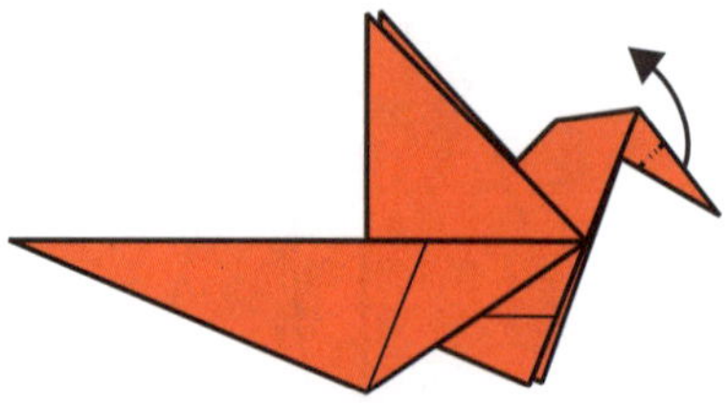

Inside reverse fold

16

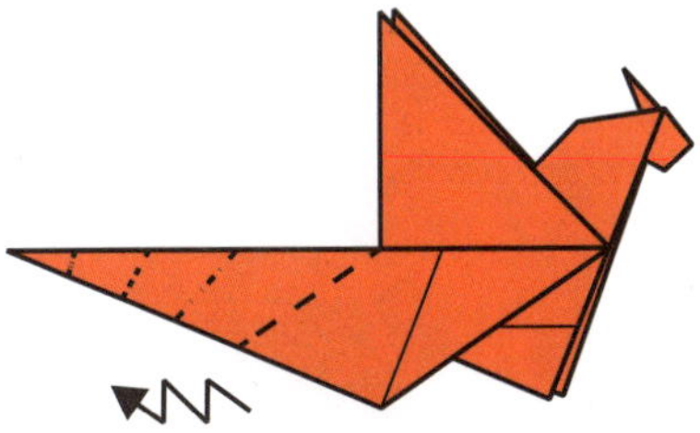

Pleat fold

17

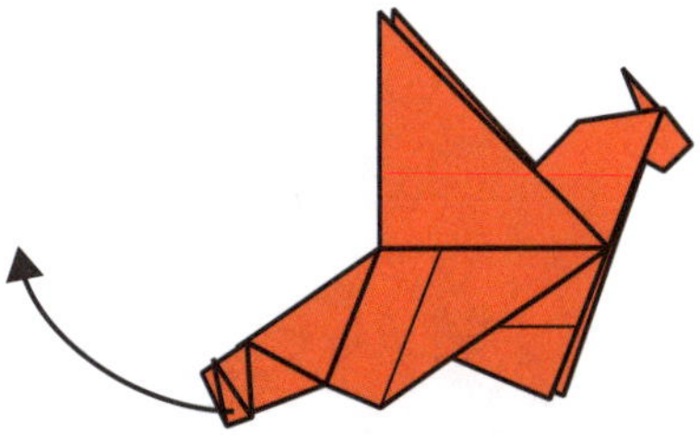

Unfold

18

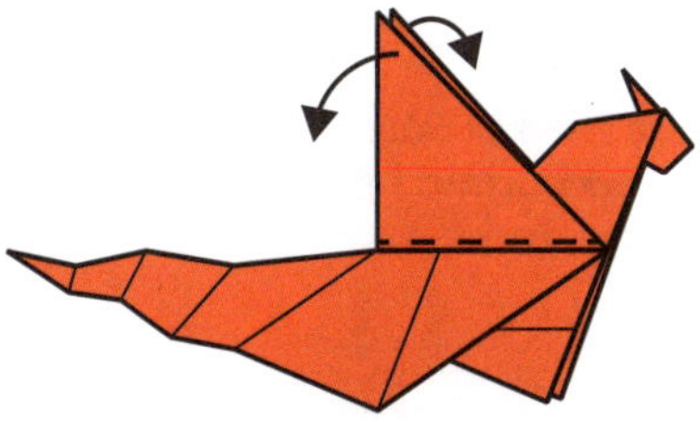

Fold down flap
Repeat behind

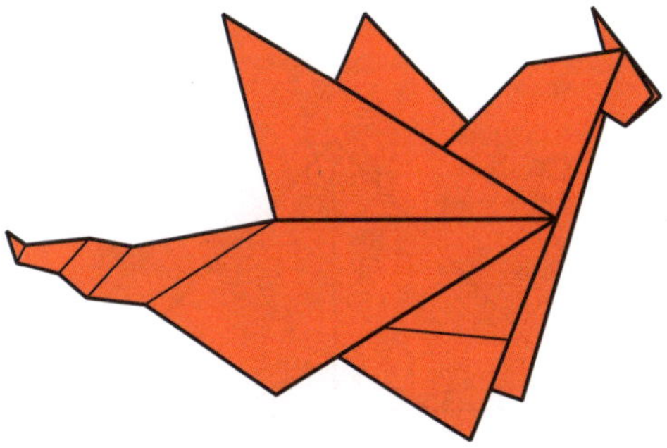

Dragon

Shark

- Diagonal Fold
- Kite Fold
- Pleat Fold
- Rabbit-ear Fold
- Inside Crimp Fold

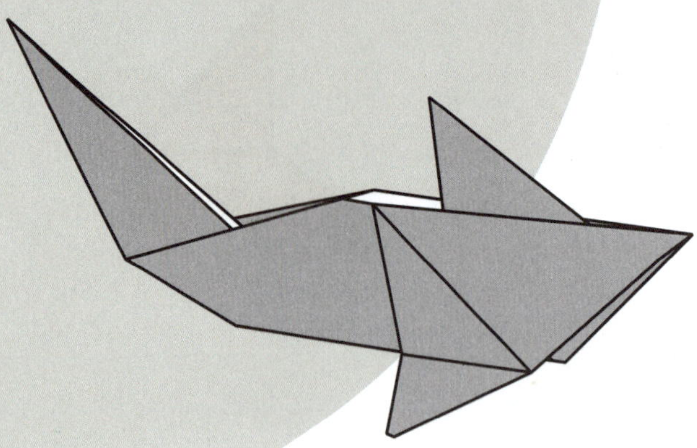

1

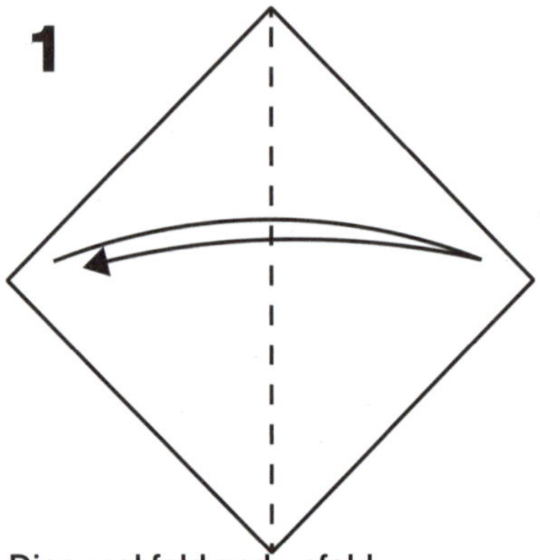

Diagonal fold and unfold

2

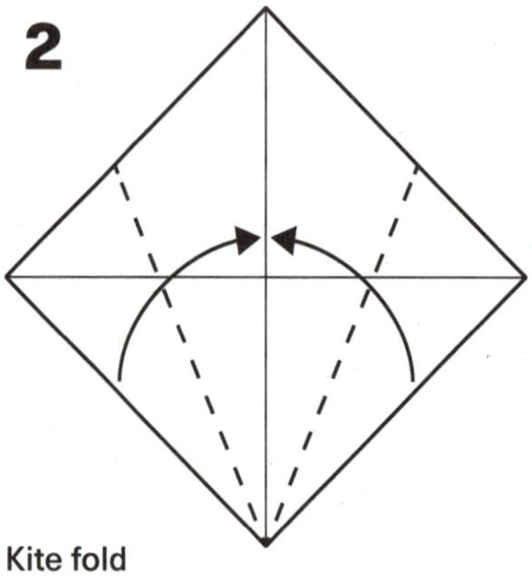

Kite fold

3

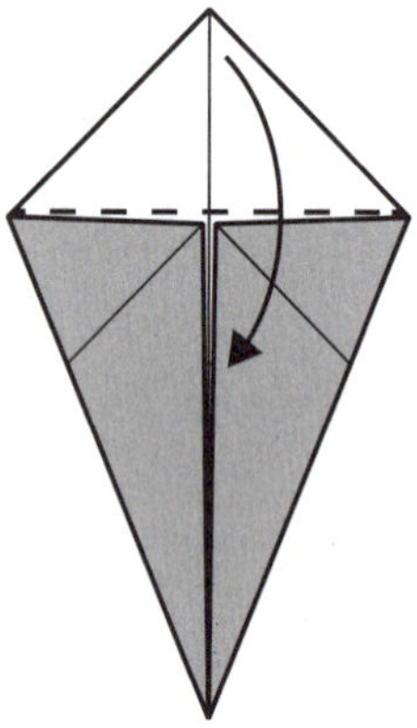

4

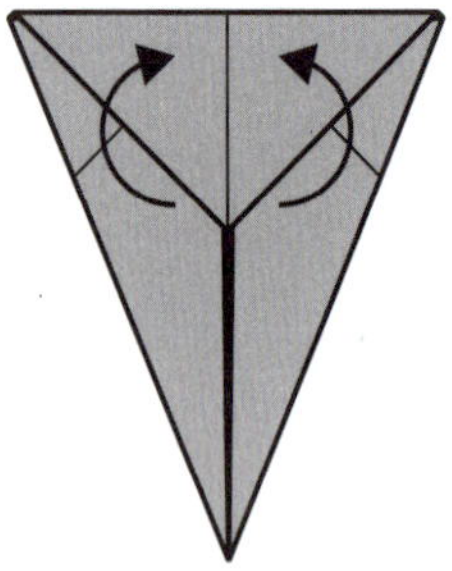

Bring flaps to front

5

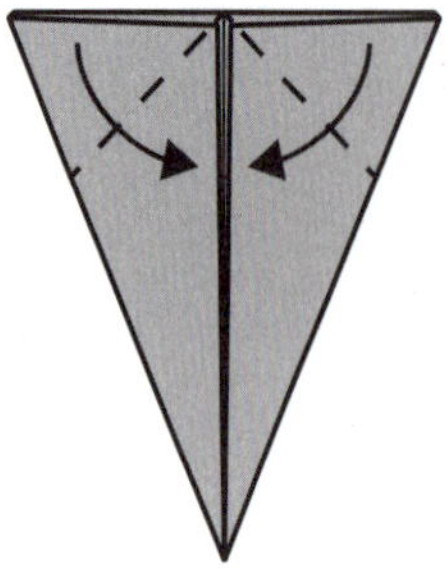

Kite fold

6

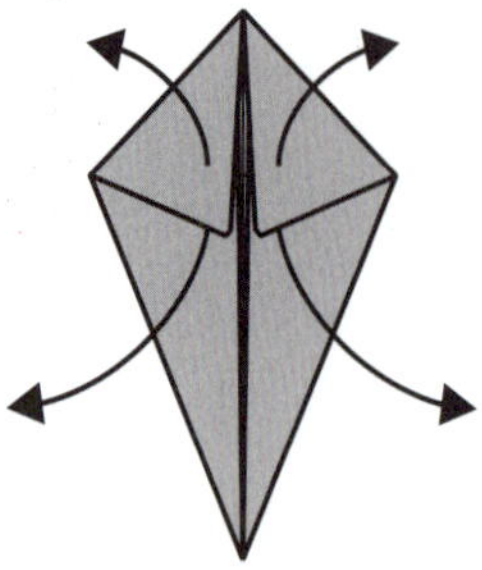

Unfold kite folds

7

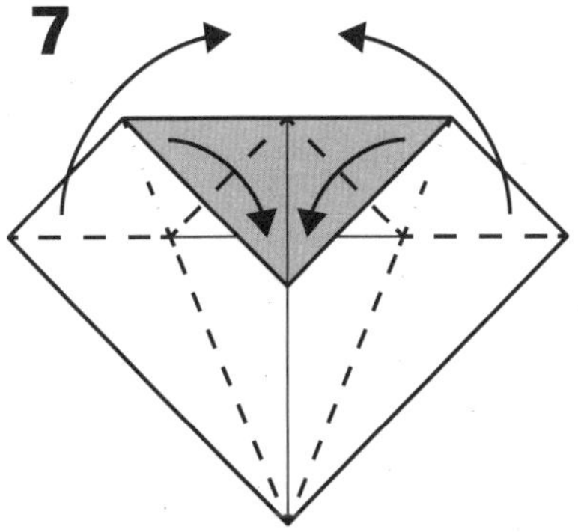

Rabbit-ear both sides

8

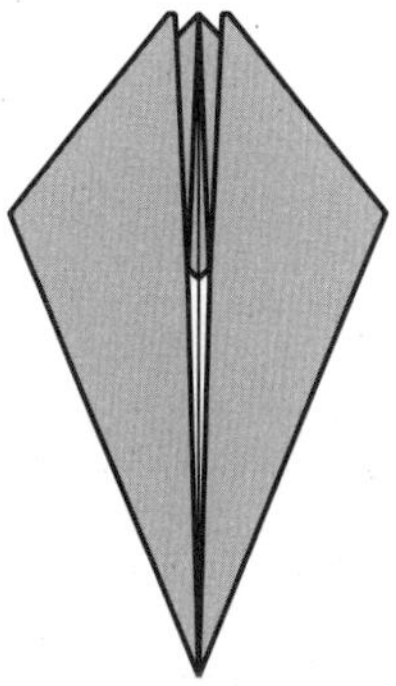

Rotate

9

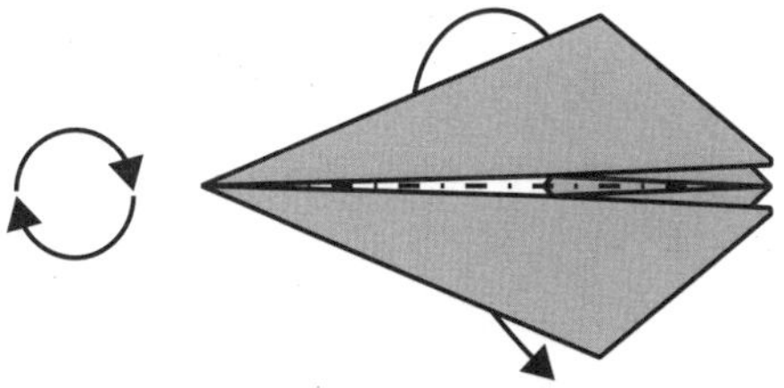

Fold in half behind

10

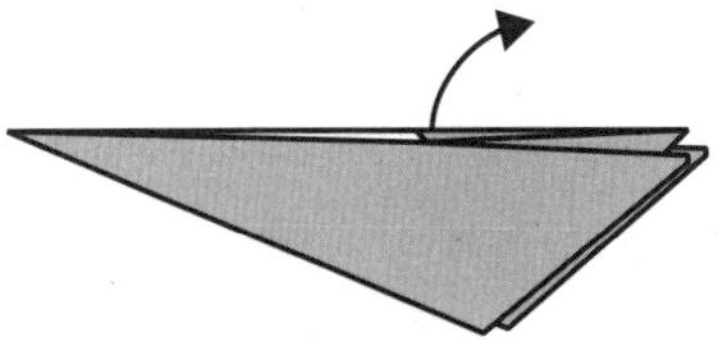

Slide up center section

11

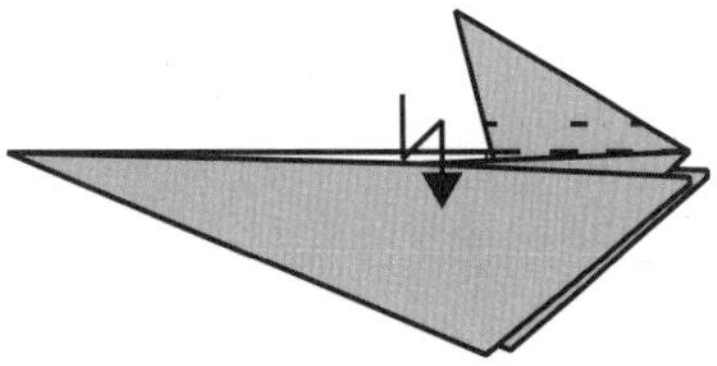

Pleat fold

12

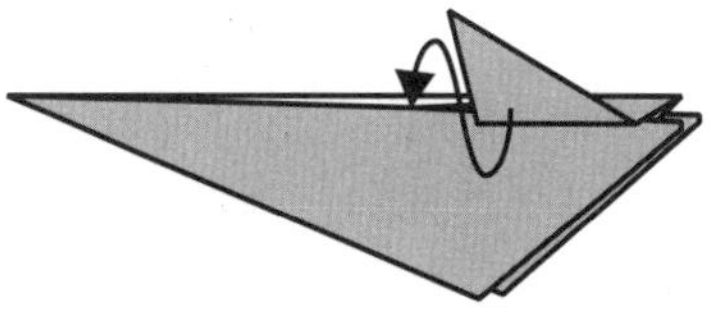

Tuck inside

13

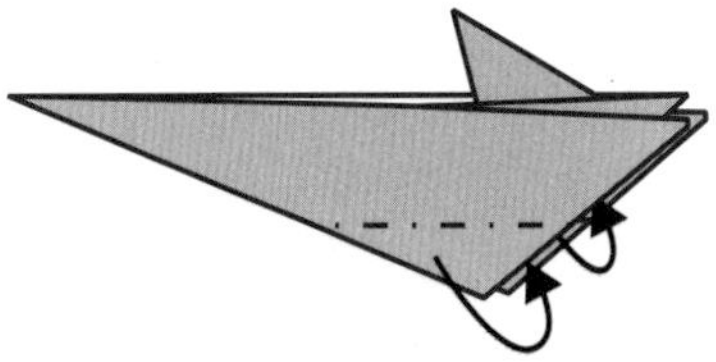

Repeat behind

14

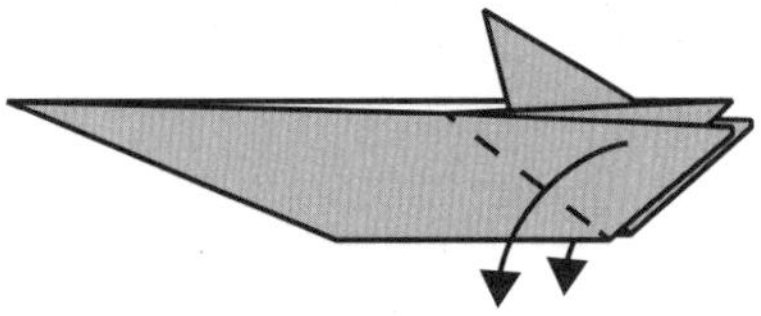

Repeat behind

15

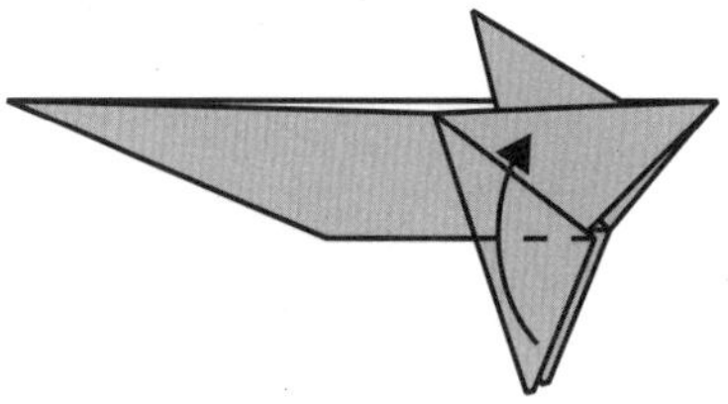

Repeat behind

16

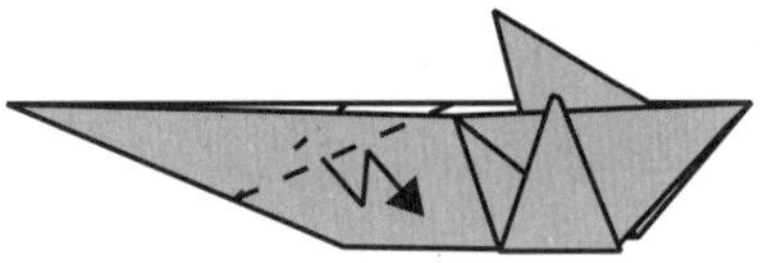

Pleat fold

17

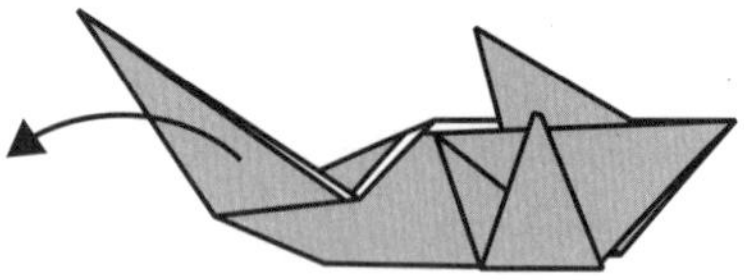

Unfold

18

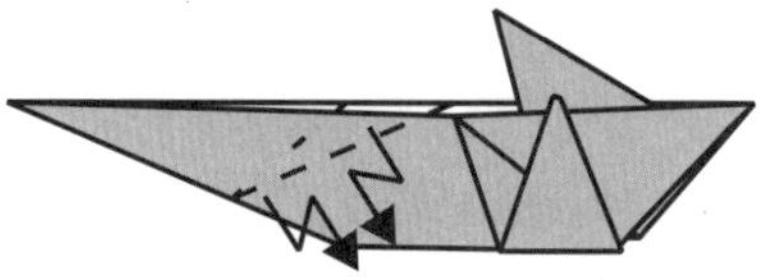

Inside crimp fold

19

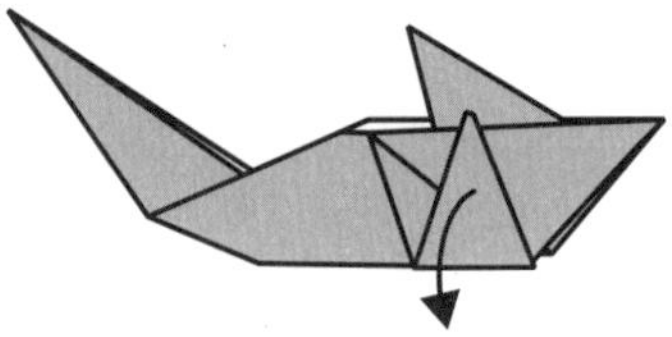

Unfold
Repeat behind

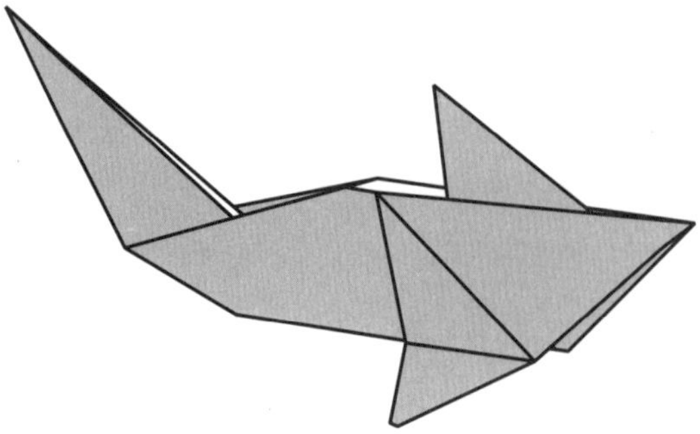

Shark

Rooster

- Diagonal Fold
- Pleat Fold
- Rabbit-ear Fold
- Fish Base
- Outside Reverse Fold
- Inside Crimp Fold

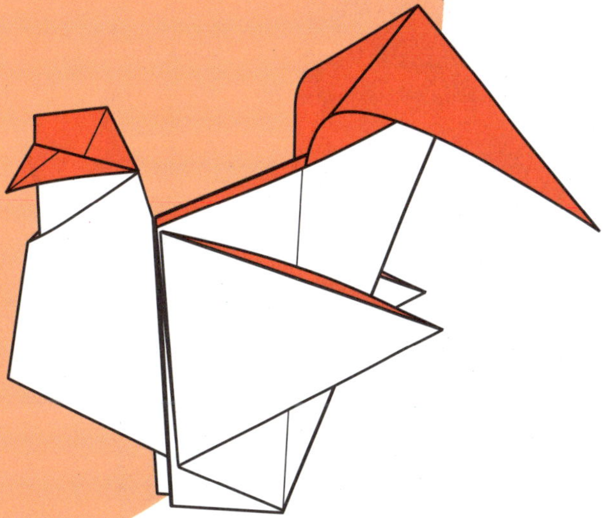

1

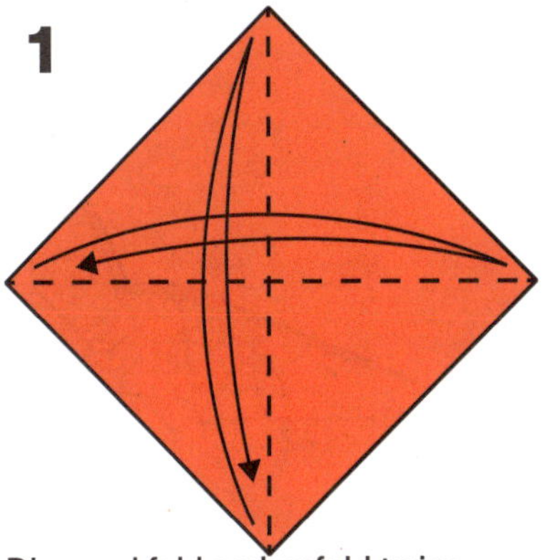

Diagonal fold and unfold twice

2

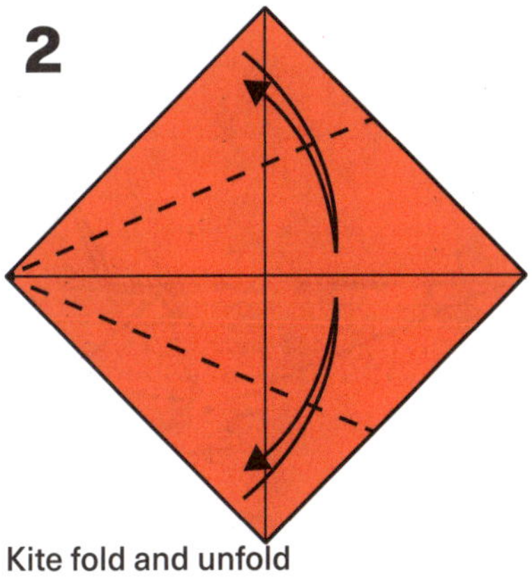

Kite fold and unfold

3

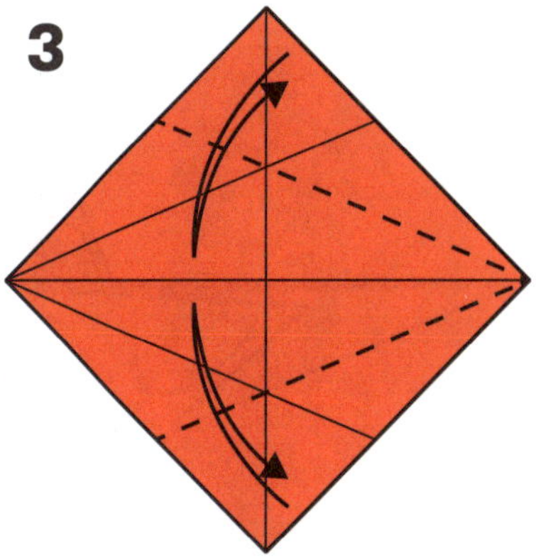

4

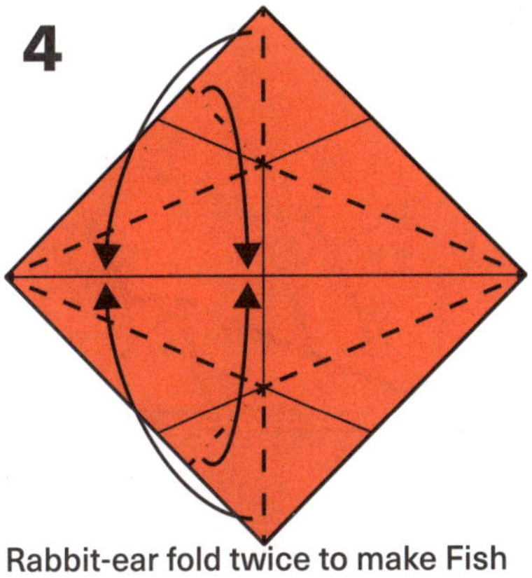

Rabbit-ear fold twice to make Fish Base

5

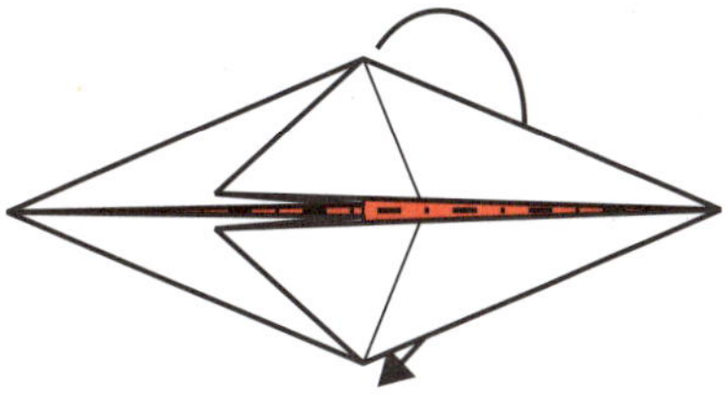

Fold in half behind

6

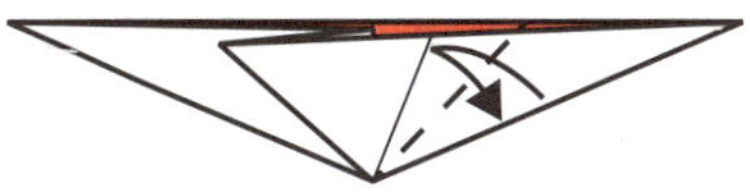

Fold to crease and unfold

7

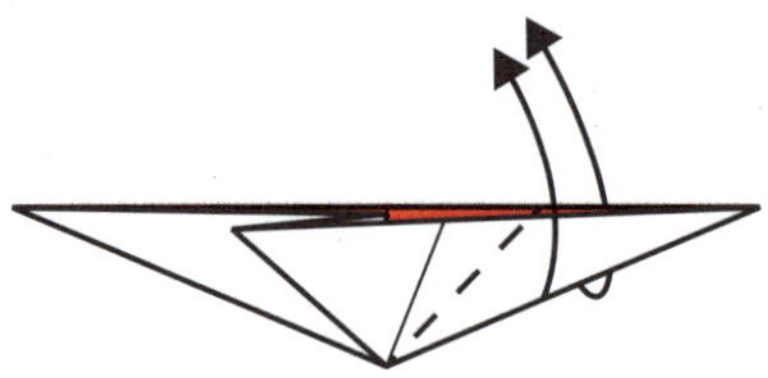

Outside reverse fold

8

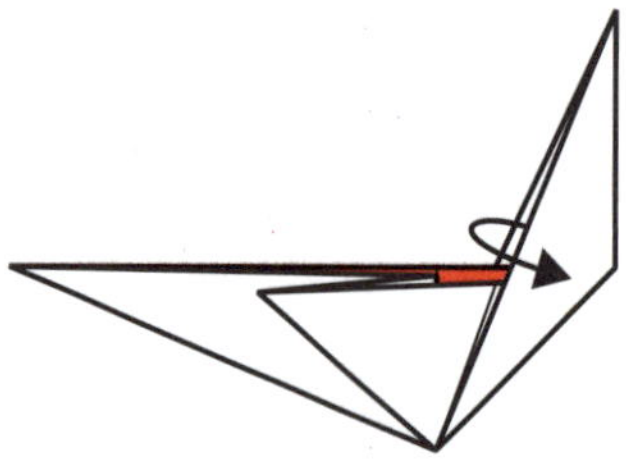

Pull out hidden layers and re-collapse on top

9

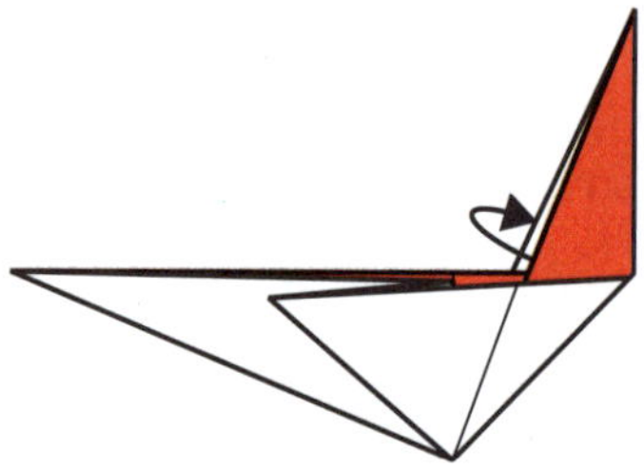

Repeat Step 8 behind

10

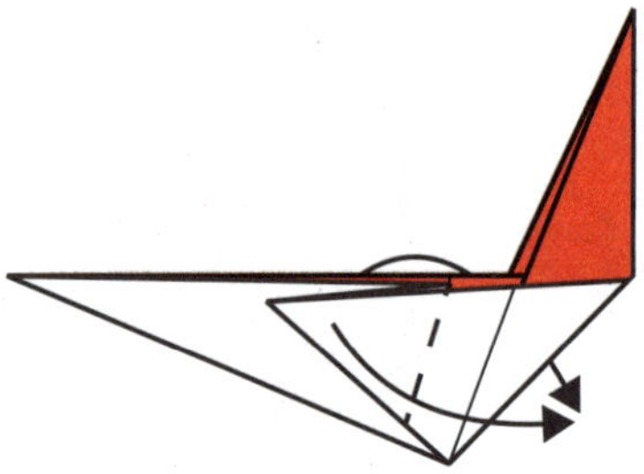

Repeat behind

11

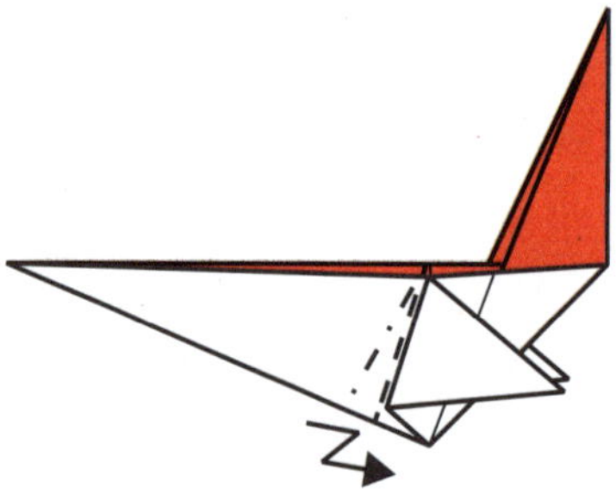

Pleat fold

12

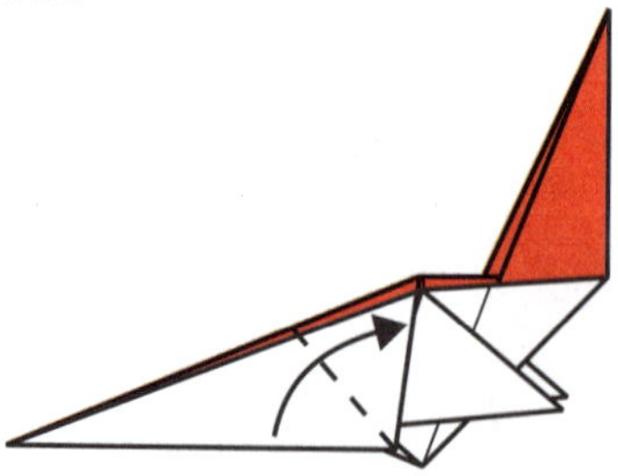

Fold edge to edge

13

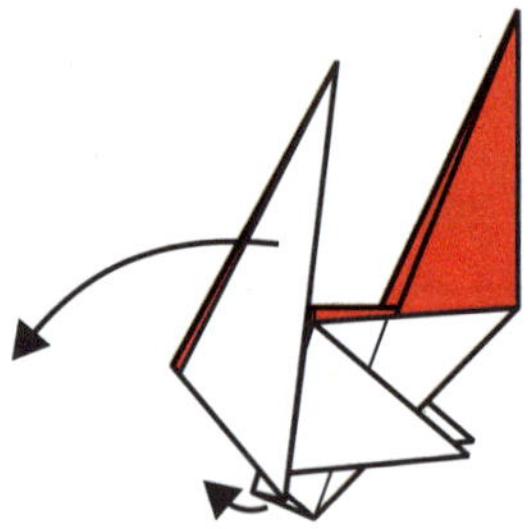

Unfold Steps 11 and 12

14

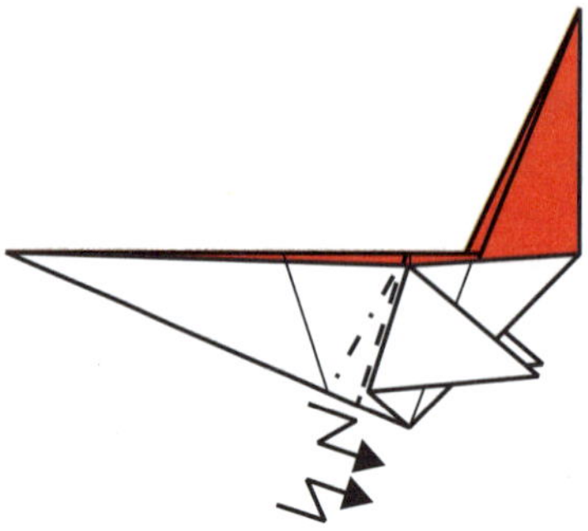

Inside crimp fold

15

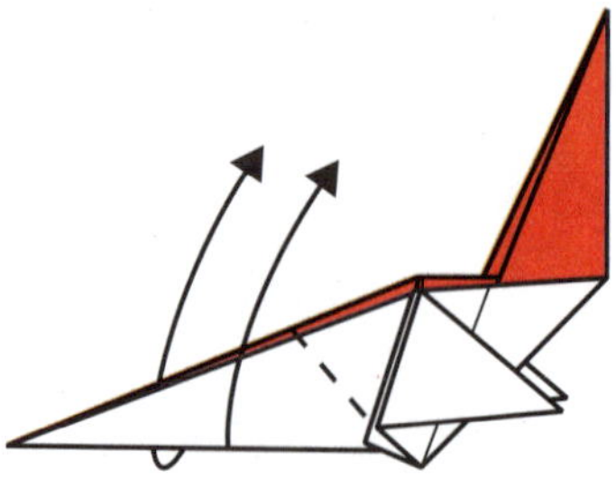

Outside reverse fold

16

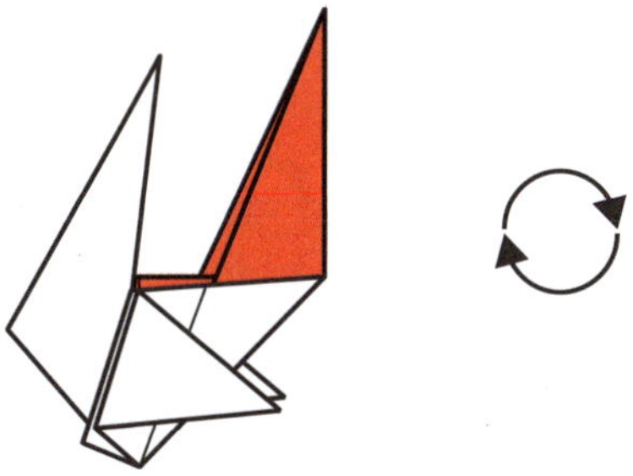

Rotate

17

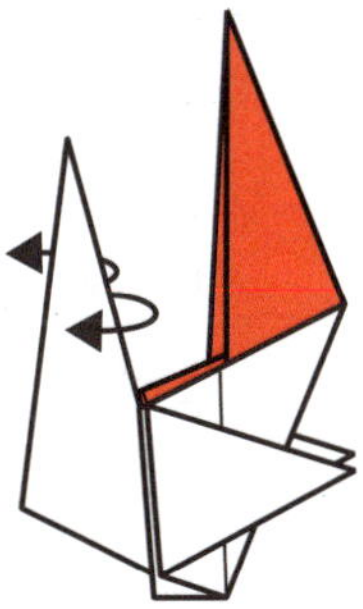

Open hidden layers

18

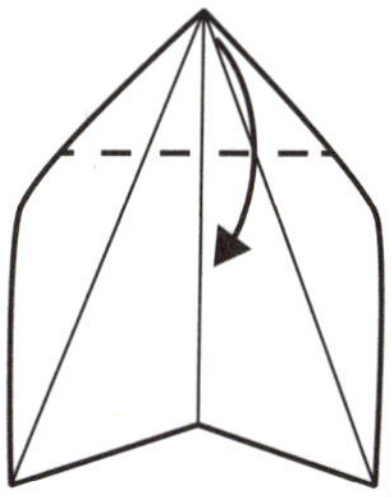

Enlarged front view shown

19

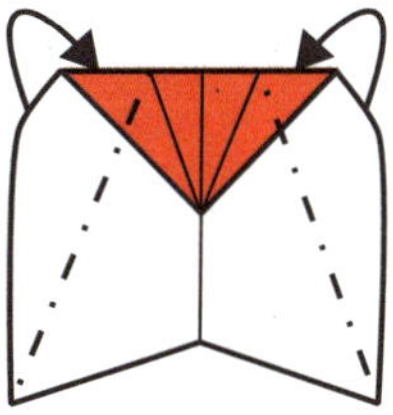

20

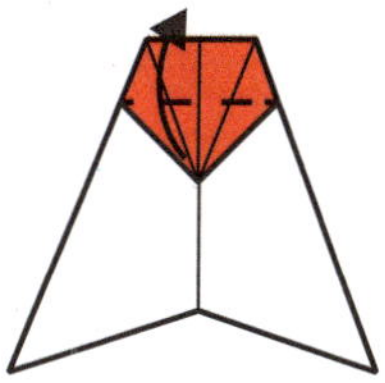

21

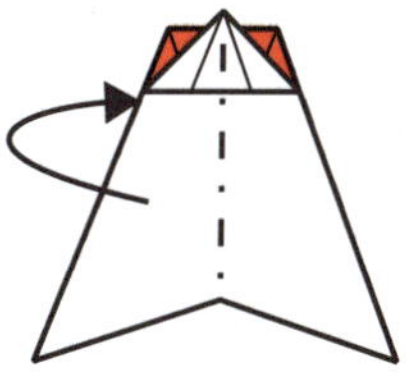

Re-collapse flat

22

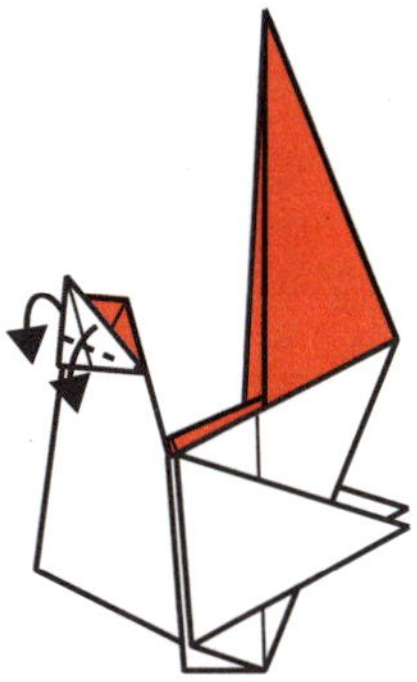

Outside reverse fold

23

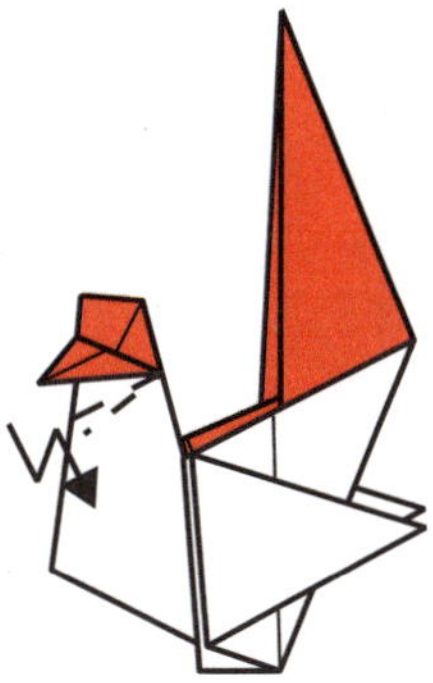

Pleat fold

24

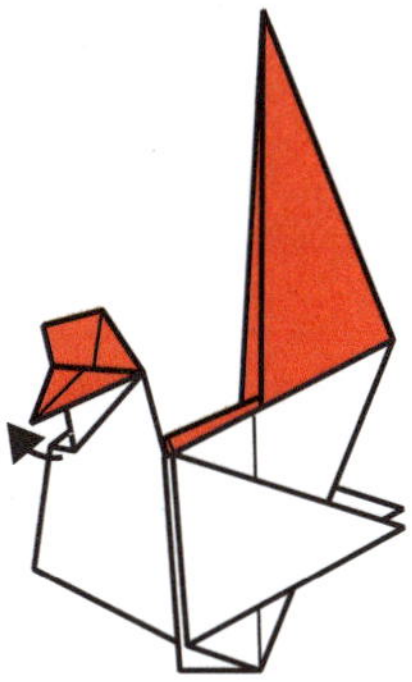

Unfold

25

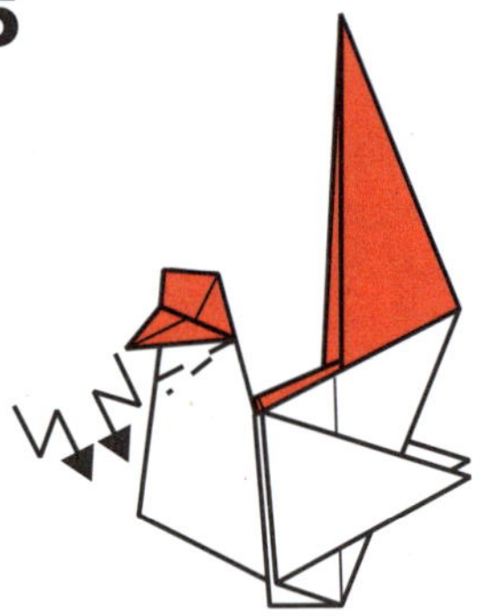

Inside crimp fold

26

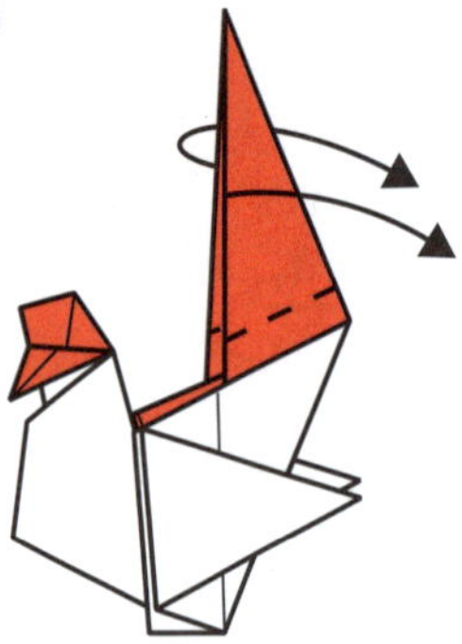

Outside reverse fold

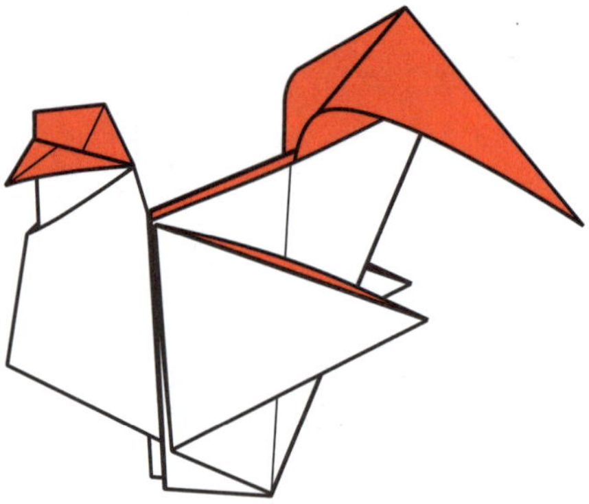

Rooster